What is History, Geography, and Prophecy?

SonLight Education Ministry
United States of America

A Suggested Daily Schedule

(Adapt this schedule to your family needs.)

5:00 a.m.	Arise–Personal Worship
6:00 a.m.	Family Worship and Bible Class–With Father
7:00 a.m.	Breakfast
8:00 a.m.	Practical Arts*–Domestic Activities 　　　　　　　Agriculture 　　　　　　　Industrial Arts 　　　　　　　(especially those related to 　　　　　　　the School Lessons)
10:00 a.m.	School Lessons (Take a break for some physical exercise during this time slot.)
12:00 p.m.	Dinner Preparations (Health class could be included at this time or a continued story.)
1:00 p.m.	Dinner
2:00 p.m.	Practical Arts* or Fine Arts (Music and Crafts) (especially those related to the School Lessons)
5:00 p.m.	Supper
6:00 p.m.	Family Worship–Father (Could do History Class)
7:00 p.m.	Personal time with God–Bed Preparation
8:00 p.m.	Bed

*Daily nature walk can be in morning or afternoon.

The Desire of All Nations

This book is a part of a curriculum that is built upon the life of Christ entitled, "The Desire of All Nations," for grades 2-8. Any of the books in this curriculum can be used by themselves or as an entire program.

INFORMATION ABOUT THE 2-8 GRADE PROGRAM

Multi-level

This program is written on a multi-level. That means that each booklet has material for grades 2-8. This is so the whole family in these grades may work from the same books. It is difficult for a busy mother to have 2 or more children and each have a different set of books. Remember, the Bible is written for all ages.

The Bible—the Primary Textbook

The books in this program are designed to teach the parent and the student how to learn academic subjects by using the Bible as a primary textbook.

The Desire of Ages

The Desire of Ages by Ellen G. White is used as a textbook to go with the Bible. This focuses on the early life of Christ, when He was a child. Children relate best to Christ as a child and youth.

Lesson Numbers

The big number in the top right corner on the cover of this book is the Lesson Number and corresponds with the chapter number in the book *The Desire of Ages*. For example, Lesson 1 in the school program will go along with chapter 1 in *The Desire of Ages*. Usually each family starts at the beginning with Lesson 1. Most children have not had a true Bible program, therefore they need the foundation built. If there is academic material that they have already covered, they do the Bible part and review then pass quickly on.

Seven Academic Subjects

There are seven academic subjects in this program—Health, Mathematics, Music, Science–Nature, History/Geography/Prophecy, Language, Voice–Speech.

Language Program

A good, solid language program is recommended to be used along with the SonLight materials.

The Riggs Institute has a multi-sensory teaching method that accommodates every child's unique learning style. Their program is called *Writing and Spelling Road to Reading and Thinking*. Order by calling (800) 200-4840 or visit www.riggsinst.org. (Disclaimer: SonLight does not endorse the reading books recommended in the Riggs' program.)

Another option which you might find more user friendly and is similar to the Riggs program but from a Christian perspective is *Spell to Write and Read* by Wanda Sanseri. To order, call Wanda Sanseri at (503) 654-2300 or visit https://www.bhibooks.net/swr.html

"God With Us"
Lesson 1 – Love

The following books are those you will need for this lesson.
All of these can be obtained from www.sonlighteducation.com

The Rainbow Covenant – Study the spiritual meaning of colors and make your own rainbow book.

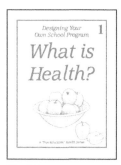

Health
What is Health?

Math
What is Mathematics?

Music
What is Music?

Science/Nature
What is Nature?

A Casket – Coloring book and story. Learn how to treat the gems of the Bible.

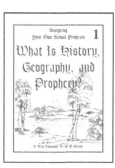

H/G/P
What is History, Geography and Prophecy?

Language
What is Language?

Speech/Voice
What is the Voice?

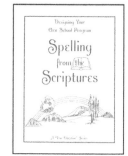

Spelling from the Scriptures

Bible Study – Learn how to study the Bible and helpful use tools.

Bible
*The Desire of all Nations I
Teacher Study Guide*

Student Study Guide

Bible Lesson Study Guide

Memory Verses
*The Desire of all Nations I
Scripture Songs Book*

and MP3 files

Our Nature Study Book – Your personal nature journal.

Outline of "The Desire of all Nations" Lesson 1

Bible	Health	Math	Music	Nature	H/G/P	Language	Voice

Week 1 | **Month 1**

Lesson 1

Day 1

Family Morning Worship *Covenant Notebook* (1) Music, Prayer, MV (2) Read pages 1-2 in the "Covenant Notebook" and discuss. (3) Sometime during the day, take a nature walk looking for rainbows. (4) Begin finding pictures of complete rainbows to put into the plastic sheets behind the "Rainbows" page. Read and discuss the "Rainbows" page.

Use these songs during this week, "All Things Bright & Beautiful," "This is My Father's World," and "We Shall Know." Find this music in *Christ in Song* book which is included in these materials under the title "Song Books."

READ THIS BEFORE BEGINNING

Cover the Teacher's Section of each school book before beginning that subject.

It is best to cover only a few concepts at once and understand them well and not run a marathon with a young person's mind. If this outline moves to fast for you SLOW down. <u>Teach one idea and teach it well!</u>

This school program is not a race with time, rather it is an experience with God. The parents are to represent their Father in Heaven before the children—students. Together learn about the Character Qualities and help one another in a godly manner to reach the finish line together.

INSTRUCTIONS

Day 2

(1) Music, Prayer, MV (2) Read page 3 in the "Covenant Notebook" and discuss. (Also use page 7)

Lay out Lesson 1 of the School Program showing the the front covers of each book, *What is Health?, What is Mathematics?, What is Music?, What is Nature?*

What is H/G/P?, What is Language?, and What is Voice?. Each book will have a color cover of one of the colors of the rainbow. Place them in order as the rainbow colors

deomonstrate in a picture. Refer to page 7 of the *Covenant Notebook* to see what each color means and how it relates to the subject that bears that color.

(Examples: Health = Christ sacrificed His body on the cross for you.

Mathematics = Deals in numbers saved and lost.

Music = Right music can turn our thoughts from things of this world to Divinity.

Nature = Right growth in character.

H/G/P = The history of obedience and disobedience; geography of lands where the gospel is to be spread; prophecy telling us the future of those keeping the law.

Language and Voice = How God's royal people should write, speak, and act to prepare for His kingdom.

Bible	Health	Math	Music	Nature	H/G/P	Language	Voice

(3) Sometime during the day take a nature walk looking for rainbows.

(4) Begin finding pictures of complete rainbows to put into the plastic sheets behind the "Rainbows" page. Read and discuss the "Rainbows" page.

Day 3-4

(1) Music, Prayer, MV

(2) Read pages 4-9 in the "Covenant Notebook" and discuss.

(3) Sometime during the day take a nature walk looking for white items (or the color pages).

(4) Begin finding pictures of white things in nature to put into the plastic sheets behind the "White" page. Read and discuss the "White" page.

Day 5

Review what you have learned.

INSTRUCTIONS

Once the white page is completed then move on to the red page and so forth, always finding things from nature for your pictures. And on your nature walks take fine the color you are currently working on. Do not look for man made things! Before going on the nature walk each day, read and discuss the information in the color section.

After day 5, and reviewing only what you have learned to that point, plan only to work on the *Covenant Notebook* one day a week until that book is finished (Use time in the afternoon and not during the regular school hours). However, do not forget to review the *Covenant Notebook* when you deem it necessary, and if you should find a new picture for it, stop and put it into *Covenant Notebook*. It gives you an opportunity to review lessons with the children.

Lesson 12 of Nature in this series is about the rainbow and would be a wonderful time to make a recommitment to God.

This *Covenant Notebook* is to prepare you for the 2-8 School Lessons. On week 2 begin the School Lessons.

Bible	Health	Math	Music	Nature	H/G/P	Language	Voice
		START THE 2-8 PROGRAM, "The Desire Of All Nations."					
Week 2 Lesson 1 **Day 1** "God With Us" (1) Music ("O Come, O come, Immanuel," "I Love Thee," "Thou didst Leave Thy Throne"), Prayer, MV (Mt 1:21) (2) Read and discuss Ge 3:14-15; 12:1-3. Discuss the Character Quality.	**Day 1** *What Is Health?* (1) Open Bibles and read II Sa 20:9. (2) Read or tell information. Do pages 1-17 or what you can cover. Discuss.	**Day 1** *What Is Math...?* (1) Open Bibles and read Mt 11:29. (2) Read or tell information. Do pages 1-8 or what you can cover. Discuss.				**Day 1** *Writing and Spelling Road to Reading and Thinking* (*WSRRT*) (1) Do your daily assignments for *WSRRT*. If you are still working on this program continue until you finish at least the 2nd teacher's notebook.	

vii

INSTRUCTIONS

If you are still using the *Family Bible Lessons* do them for one of your worships each day and use *The Desire of all Nations* for the other worship each day.

These are the items you will need for worship for *The Desire of all Nations* Bible program: Old King James Bible (**NOT** the New King James Bible)
"*The Desire of all Nations*," Volume 1, Study Guide for the KJV Bible Lessons
The Desire of all Nations Teacher and Student Study Guides #1 (Chapters from *The Desire of Ages* Bible text book)
The Desire of all Nations Song Book #1 and CD Music #1 for Memory Verses
Christ in Song Song Book #1, 2, 3, 4

These are the items you will need for class time:

What is Health?; What is Mathematics?; What is Music?; What is Nature?; What is H/G/P?; What is Language?; and What is Voice?.
Our Nature Study Book "The Casket" Story & Coloring Book
Bible Study
Road Map and Route Catalogue

Bible	Health	Math	Music	Nature	H/G/P	Language	Voice
Day 2 "God With Us" (1) Music ("O Come, O come, Immanuel," "I Love Thee," "Thou didst Leave Thy Throne"), Prayer, MV (Mt 1:21; Jn 8:28) (2) Read and discuss Gal 3:16; Ge 49:10; De 18:17-19; II Sam 7:12-17.	**Day 2** *What Is Health?* (1) Open Bibles and read I Co 12:23. (2) Read or tell information. Do pages 18-26 or what you can cover. Discuss.	**Day 2** *What Is Math...?* (1) Open Bibles and read Luke 6:38; Is 40:12; Ps 147:4; Is 40:26; Job 28:25. (2) Read or tell information. Do pages 9-22 or what you can cover. Discuss. **END**				**Day 2** *Writing and Spelling Road to Reading and Thinking* (1) Do your daily assignments for *WSRRT*.	
Day 3 "God With Us" (1) Music, Prayer, MV (Mt 1:21; Jn 8:28) (2) Read and discuss Ez 21:25-27; Lu 1:32, Isa 9:6-7.	**Day 3** *What Is Health?* (1) Open Bibles and read Pr 26:2. (2) Read or tell information. Do pages 27-35 or what you can cover. Discuss.		**Day 3** *What Is Music?* (1) Open Bibles and read Zeph 3:17. (2) Read or tell information. Do pages 1-6 or what you can cover. Discuss.			**Day 3** *Writing and Spelling Road to Reading and Thinking* (1) Do your daily assignments for *WSRRT*.	
Day 4 "God With Us" (1) Review what you have already covered.	**Day 4** *What Is Health?* (1) Review pages 1-35.	**Day 4** *What Is Math...?* (1) Review.	**Day 4** *What Is Music?* (1) Open Bibles and read Re 14:2-3. (2) Read or tell information. Do pages 7-17 or what you can cover. Discuss.			**Day 4** *Writing and Spelling Road to Reading and Thinking* (1) Do your daily assignments for *WSRRT*.	
Day 5	**Day 5**	**Day 5**	**Day 5**			**Day 5** Review	

Find practical applications from your textbooks you have thus far used this week. You will find them listed under "**Reinforce**." Choose and use today.

Bible	Health	Math	Music	Nature	H/G/P	Language	Voice
Week 3 Lesson 1 **Day 1** "God With Us" (1) Music, Prayer, MV (Mt 1:21; Jn 8:28) (2) Read and discuss Ps 45:1-8; 72:1-11; Is 53.	**Day 1** *What Is Health?* (1) Open Bibles and read James 5:14. (2) Read or tell information. Do pages 36-39 or what you can cover. Discuss.		**Day 1** *What Is Music?* (1) Open Bibles and read I Ki 19:12. (2) Read or tell information. Do pages 18-30 or what you can cover. Discuss.			**Day 1** *Writing and Spelling Road to Reading and Thinking* (1) Do your daily assignments for *WSRRT.*	
Day 2 "God With Us" (1) Music, Prayer, MV (Mt 1:21; Jn 8:28; Jn 8:50) (2) Read and discuss Zec 12:10; Jn 14:9; Mt 1:23; Jn 1:1-4.	**Day 2** *What Is Health?* (1) Open Bibles and read De 34:7. (2) Read or tell information. Do pages 40-44 or what you can cover. Discuss.		**Day 2** *What Is Music?* (1) Open Bibles and read I Chr 13:8. (2) Read or tell information. Do pages 31-52 or what you can cover. Discuss. END			**Day 2** *Writing and Spelling Road to Reading and Thinking* (1) Do your daily assignments for *WSRRT.*	
Day 3 "God With Us" (1) Music, Prayer, MV (Mt 1:21; Jn 8:28; Jn 8:50; Phil 2:5-11) (2) Read and discuss *The Desire of Ages* 19-20:0.	**Day 3** *What Is Health?* (1) Open Bibles and read Ez 33:11. (2) Read or tell information. Do pages 45-53 or what you can cover. Discuss.			**Day 3** *What Is Nature?* (1) Open Bibles and read Ro 13:10. (2) Read or tell information. Do pages 1-11 or what you can cover. Discuss.		**Day 3** *Writing and Spelling Road to Reading and Thinking* (1) Do your daily assignments for *WSRRT.*	

Bible	Health	Math	Music	Nature	H/G/P	Language	Voice
Day 4 "God With Us" (1) Music, Prayer, MV (Mt 1:21; Jn 8:28; Jn 8:50; Phil 2:5-11) (2) Read and discuss *The Desire of Ages* 20:2-21:0.	**Day 4** *What Is Health?* (1) Open Bibles and read De 7:15; De 32:46; and Pr 4:20, 22. (2) Read or tell information. Do pages 54-60 or what you can cover. Discuss.			**Day 4** *What Is Nature?* (1) Open Bibles and read Ps 40:5; Ps 111:4. (2) Read or tell information. Do pages 12-17 or what you can cover. Discuss.		**Day 4** *Writing and Spelling Road to Reading and Thinking* (1) Do your daily assignments for *WSRRT*.	
Day 5 "God With Us" (1) Review.	**Day 5** *What Is Health?* (1) Review pages 1-60.	**Day 5** *What Is Math...?* (1) Review.	**Day 5** *What Is Music?* (1) Review.	**Day 5** *What Is Nature?* (1) Review pages 1-17.		**Day 5** *Writing and Spelling Road to Reading and Thinking* (1) Do your daily assignments for *WSRRT*.	
Week 4 Lesson 1 **Day 1** "God With Us" (1) Music, Prayer, MV (Mt 1:21; Jn 8:28; Jn 8:50; Phil 2:5-11) (2) Read and discuss *The Desire of Ages* 21:1-2.	**Day 1** *What Is Health?* (1) Open Bibles and read De 7:15; De 32:46; and Pr 4:20, 22. (2) Read the story. Do pages 61-80. Discuss.			**Day 1** *What Is Nature?* (1) Open Bibles and read Job 12:7-8. (2) Read or tell information. Do pages 18-23 or what you can cover. Discuss.		**Day 1** *Writing and Spelling Road to Reading and Thinking* (1) Do your daily assignments for *WSRRT*.	
Day 2 "God With Us" (1) Music, Prayer, MV (Mt 1:21; Jn 8:28; Jn 8:50; Phil 2:5-11) (2) Read and discuss *The Desire of Ages* 21:3-22:1.	**Day 2** *What Is Health* (1) Open Bibles and review De 7:15; De 32:46; and Pr 4:20, 22. (2) Do pages 81-86. Discuss. END			**Day 2** *What Is Nature?* (1) Open Bibles and read Ps 143:5. (2) Read or tell information. Do pages 24-30 or what you can cover. END		**Day 2** *WSRRT* (1) Do your daily assignments for *WSRRT*. Continue the *WSRRT* but add the Language lessons in whenever it is time to do them. **This will not be repeated.**	

Bible	Health	Math	Music	Nature	H/G/P	Language	Voice
Day 3 "God With Us" (1) Music, Prayer, MV (Mt 1:21; Jn 8:28; Jn 8:50; Phil 2:5-11) (2) Read and discuss *The Desire of Ages* 21:3-22:3.					**Day 3** *What Is H/G/P?* (1) Open Bibles and read He 1:10. (2) Read or tell information. Do pages 1-6 or what you can cover. Discuss. Choose a good mission book to begin reading as a family.	**Day 3** *What Is Language?* (1) Open Bibles and read Col 3:16. (2) Read or tell information. Do pages 1-10 or what you can cover + *WSRRT*. Discuss.	
Day 4 "God With Us" (1) Music, Prayer, MV (Mt 1:21; Jn 8:28; Jn 8:50; Phil 2:5-11) (2) Read and discuss *The Desire of Ages* 21:3-22:3.					**Day 4** *What Is H/G/P?* (1) Open Bibles and read Ps 119:105 & He 13:1. (2) Read or tell information. Do pages 7-14. Discuss.	**Day 4** *What Is Language?* (1) Open Bibles and read Pr 25:11. (2) Read or tell information. Do pages 11-17 + *WSRRT*. Discuss.	**Day 4** *What Is Voice?* (1) Open Bibles and read Ps 105:2. (2) Read or tell information. Do pages 1-4 Discuss.
Day 5 "God With Us" (1) Review. Music, Prayer, MV. (2) Read and discuss *The Desire of Ages* 22:4-24:1.	**Day 5** *What Is Health?* (1) Review	**Day 5** *What Is Math…?* (1) Review.	**Day 5** *What Is Music?* (1) Review.	**Day 5** *What Is Nature?* (1) Review.	**Day 5** *What Is H/G/P?* (1) Review pages 1-14.	**Day 5** *What Is Language?* (1) Review pages 1-17.	**Day 5** *What Is Voice?* (1) Review pages 1-4.
Week 1 (5) Month 2 **Lesson 1** **Day 1** "God With Us" (1) Music, Prayer, MV. (2) Read and discuss *The Desire of Ages* 24:2-26:3.		If there is any information that the student should know and does not—REVIEW.			**Day 1** *What Is H/G/P?* (1) Open Bibles and read Jer 10:12. (2) Read or tell information. Do pages 15-25Aa or what you can cover. Discuss.	Do your daily assignments for *WSRRT*. **Day 1** *What Is Language?* (1) Open Bibles and read Jn 1:1. (2) Read or tell information. Do pages 18-22 or what you can cover. Discuss. **END**	**Day 1** *What Is Voice?* (1) Open Bibles and read Ps 32:2. (2) Read or tell information. Do pages 5-8. Discuss. **END**

Bible	Health	Math	Music	Nature	H/G/P	Language	Voice
Day 2 "God With Us" (1) Music, Prayer, MV. (2) Expand or review any part of the lesson. (Could use section about William Miller in H/G/P.)					**Day 2** *What Is H/G/P?* (1) Open Bibles and read II Pe 1:21. (2) Read or tell information. Do pages 26-47 or what you can cover. Discuss. (Story about "William Miller" may take longer.)	**Day 2** *Writing and Spelling Road to Reading and Thinking* (1) Do your daily assignments for WSRRT.	**Day 2** *What Is Voice?* (1) Review
Day 3 "God With Us" (1) Music, Prayer, MV. (2) Expand or review any part of the lesson. (Could use the section in H/G/P, "The Schools of the Prophets.")					**Day 3** *What Is H/G/P?* (1) Open Bibles and read Ja 3:17 & Pr 9:10. (2) Read or tell information. Do pages 48-65 or what you can cover. Discuss.	**Day 3** *Writing and Spelling Road to Reading and Thinking* (1) Do your daily assignments for WSRRT.	
Day 4 "God With Us" (1) Music, Prayer, MV. (2) Expand or review any part of the lesson. (Could explain why the Apocrypha books are not included in Bible.) **END**					**Day 4** *What Is H/G/P?* (1) Open Bibles and read Ex 17:14 & Ge 5:22. (2) Read or tell information. Do pages 66-78 or what you can cover. Discuss. **END**	**Day 4** *Writing and Spelling Road to Reading and Thinking* (1) Do your daily assignments for WSRRT.	**Day 4-5** Use this time to review anything from lesson 1.

On day 5 review any subject in Lesson 1 that needs a better understanding.

Continue the process with Lesson 2. See the *Road Map and Route Catalogue.*

Week 2 [**Month 2**]
Lesson 2
Day 1 "The Chosen People" (1) Music, Prayer, MV. (2) Read and discuss.

History/Geography/Prophecy
Instruction Sheet

1. Have your student draw a map of the world on the blackboard or on paper. This will help him test his recall of the proper shapes of the countries of the world.

2. Always make spiritual parallels to the History/Geography/Prophecy lesson and character quality.

3. Remember:

History teaches us about past events.

Geography is the study of the natural features of the earth, its climate, products, and people.

Prophecy teaches us what is to come in the future.

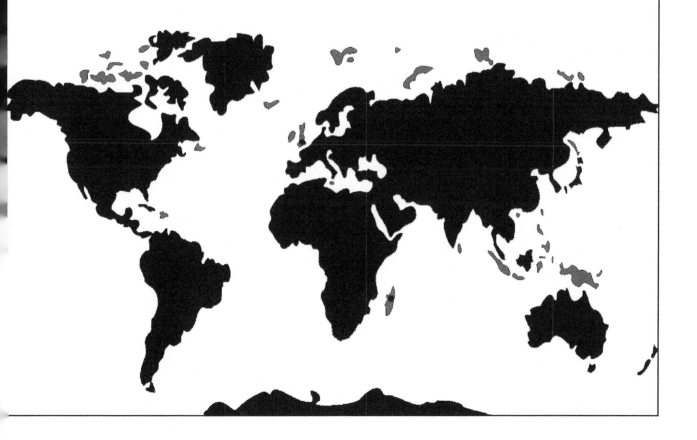

Table of Contents

Teacher Section

"Now all these things
happened unto them for ensamples:
and they are written for our admonition,
upon whom the ends of the world are come."
1 Corinthians 10:11

# INSTRUCTIONS
for the Teacher

Step 1

Study the Bible Lesson and begin to memorize the Memory Verses. Familiarize Yourself With the Character Quality. The student can answer the Bible Review Questions. See page 6. Use the Steps in Bible Study.

Bible Lesson

"God With Us" – Genesis 3:14-15; 12:1-3; Galatians 3:16; Genesis 49:10; Deuteronomy 18:17-19; II Samuel 7:12-17; Ezekiel 21:25-27; Luke 1:32; Isaiah 9:6-7; Psalm 45:1-8; 72:1-11; Isaiah 53; Zechariah 12:10; John 14:9; Matthew 1:23; John 1:1-4; Matthew 1:23

Memory Verses

Matthew 1:23; Matthew 1:20-21; John 8:28; 6:57; 7:18; 8:50; Philippians 2:5-11

Character Quality

Love – an affection of the mind excited by beauty and worth of any kind, or by the qualities of an object; charity

Antonyms – hate; detestableness; abomination; loathing; scorn; disdainfulness; selfishness

Character Quality Verse

I Corinthians 13:4-7 – *"Charity suffereth long, and is kind; charity envieth not; charity vaunteth not itself, is not puffed up,*

"Doth not behave itself unseemly, seeketh not her own, is not easily provoked, thinketh no evil;

"Rejoiceth not in iniquity, but rejoiceth in the truth;

"Beareth all things, believeth all things, hopeth all things, endureth all things."

Step 2

Understand How To/And

A. Do the Spelling Cards so the student can begin to build his own spiritual dictionary.

B. Mark the Bible.

C. Evaluate Your Student's Character in relation to the character quality of **love**.

D. Familiarize Yourself with H/G/P. Notice the Projects.

E. Review the Scripture References for "H/G/P."

F. Notice the Answer Key.

A. Spelling Cards
Spelling Lists

H/G/P Words
Place I - II - III

history	future
geography	School of the
prophecy	Prophets
footprints	walking

Bible Words

blessing	heel	Prophet
bruise	Judah	scepter
Emmanuel	kingdom	seed
enmity	lawgiver	Shiloh
forever	**love**	throne
head	peace	woman

See the booklet
Spelling from the Scriptures **for instructions.**

B. How to Mark the Bible

1. Copy the list of Bible texts in the back of the Bible on an empty page as a guide.

2. Go to the first text in the Bible and copy the next text beside it. Go to the next one and repeat the process until they are all chain referenced.

3. Have the student present the study to family and/or friends.

4. In each student lesson there is one or more sections that have a Bible marking study on the subject studied. (See the student's section, pages 77-78.)

C. Evaluate Your Student's Character

This section is for the purpose of helping the teacher know how to encourage the students in becoming more **loving**. See page 4.

Place I = Grades 2-3-4
Place II = Grades 4-5-6
Place III = Grades 6-7-8

D. Familiarize Yourself With History, Geography, and Prophecy – Notice the Projects

Projects

1. **History** – Have the child think of an act of **love** done to him this past week.

Geography – Have the child think of that person and return the act of **love** by sending a card to him.

Prophecy – Have the child plan for the future to do something for another person. (Examples: a special picture he draws, a craft he makes, a loaf of bread or special treat he makes, or a letter he writes.)

2. Have the child think of something from his **past** that needs improvement in his life, so in the **future** he will act in **love**. (Examples: kinder words to brother or sister, helpful spirit, etc.)

3. Have the child answer the following questions: What was the history of Jesus before He came to this earth? Find a Bible verse giving the answer.

Where is Jesus today? Explain about that heavenly land—geography.

Find a Bible verse giving the answer.

What does prophecy tell us about Jesus in the future? Find a Bible verse giving the answer.

4. Answer these questions orally and discuss. What is your child's history of the past years? Where is he living today? What is his future? (Encourage a **love** commitment to the Lord explaining that Christ's **love** provided a way to cover our past sins, He helps us overcome present weaknesses and sins; and He will come in the future and take the righteous to heaven.)

5. Make a family tree. Through this project the child will learn about family members he may not know. He will learn about his family heritage.

6. Plan a family outing to visit a family member that has not been visited by the family for a long time or maybe never.

Evaluating Your Child's Character

Check the appropriate box for your student's level of development, or your own, as the case may be.

Maturing Nicely (MN), Needs Improvement (NI), Poorly Developed (PD), Absent (A)

Love

1. *"**Charity** suffereth long and is kind"* (I Corinthians 13:4). Does my child show a maturity of **love** that enables them to be kind while suffering from hunger, tiredness, or discomfort?

MN   NI   PD   A
☐   ☐   ☐   ☐

2. When the child encounters people with character deficiencies, is the child's reaction one of **loving** pity and concern instead of condemnation?

MN   NI   PD   A
☐   ☐   ☐   ☐

3. Does your child seem to **love** God more as a result of studying the material contained in the Bible?

MN   NI   PD   A
☐   ☐   ☐   ☐

4. *"**Charity**...vaunteth not itself; is not puffed up"* (I Corinthians 13:4). Does the child refrain from comparing himself with others? Do they make comments like "I can read better than _____ ."

MN   NI   PD   A
☐   ☐   ☐   ☐

5. *"**Charity**...seeketh not her own"* (I Corinthians 13:5). Is the child willing for others to have the best or the most of desirable things?

MN   NI   PD   A
☐   ☐   ☐   ☐

6. *"**Love** your enemies"* (Matthew 5:44). Does the child initiate reconciliation with or do kind things for those who have hard feelings toward him or who have treated him unfairly?

MN   NI   PD   A
☐   ☐   ☐   ☐

7. *"**Charity** shall cover the multitude of sins"* (I Peter 4:8). Is the child eager to tell you about the failures of others or do they **lovingly** shield others from exposure where possible to do so with integrity?

MN   NI   PD   A
☐   ☐   ☐   ☐

8. *"**Charity**...thinketh no evil"* (I Corinthians 13:5). Is the child unsuspecting, every placing the most favorable construction upon the motives and acts of others?

MN   NI   PD   A
☐   ☐   ☐   ☐

E. Review the Scripture References for "H/G/P"

Teacher, read through this section before working on the lesson with the student.

See pages 77-78 in the Student Section.

F. Notice the Answer Key

The Answer Key for the student book is found on page 9.

Step 3

Read the Lesson Aim.

Lesson Aim

This lesson is to give the child an introduction to "What is History, Geography, and Prophecy?" It will help him understand the character quality of **love** through the lesson, "God With Us."

History tells us about the past. Geography teaches us about the earth's surface, climate, continents, countries, peoples, industries, and products and the way they affect one another in the past, in the present, and in the future. Prophecy teaches us what is to come in the future.

The Bible prophesied of Jesus coming to this world, " *'His name shall be called Immanuel...God with us.' 'The light of the knowledge of the glory of God'* is seen *'in the face of Jesus Christ.'* From the days of eternity the Lord Jesus Christ was one with the Father; He was *'the image of God,'* the image of His greatness and majesty, *'the outshining of his glory.'* It was to manifest this glory that He came to our world. To this sin-darkened earth He came to reveal the light of God's **love**—to be *'God with us.'* Therefore it was prophesied of Him, *'His name shall be called Immanuel.'*" (*The Desire of Ages* 19)

Jesus lived as an example for us to follow in His <u>footprints</u>. He has promised He will come again very soon to take us to His home in heaven, *"and he will dwell with them, and they shall be his people, and God himself shall be with them, and be their God."*

Step 4

Prepare to begin the H/G/P Lesson.

To Begin the H/G/P Lesson

Sit down with a family photo album and look at family pictures. Talk about the past history of the family, how to help them now, and the future in Christ.

Step 5

Begin the H/G/P lesson. Cover only what can be understood by your student. Make the lessons a family project by all being involved in part or all of the lesson. These lessons are designed for the whole family.

Steps in Bible Study

1. Prayer

2. Read the verses/meditate/memorize.

3. Look up key words in *Strong's Concordance* and find their meaning in the Hebrew or Greek dictionary in the back of that book.

4. Cross reference (marginal reference) with other Bible texts. An excellent study tool is *The Treasury of Scripture Knowledge*.

5. Use Bible custom books for more information on the times.

6. Write a summary of what you have learned from those verses.

7. Mark key thoughts in the margin of your Bible.

8. Share your study with others to reinforce the lessons you have learned.

Review Questions

1. What were the circumstances under which the first promise of a Redeemer was given? (Genesis 3:14-15)

2. What promise was made to Abraham, and what did it mean? (Genesis 12:1-3; Galatians 3:16)

3. Through what tribe of Israel was the Messiah to come? (Genesis 49:10)

4. What promise was given through Moses? (Deuteronomy 18:17-19)

5. Through whom was the permanence of David's kingdom assured? (II Samuel 7:12-17; Ezekiel 21:25-27; Luke 1:32)

6. What exalted ideas concerning the Messiah were made prominent? (Isaiah 9:6-7; Psalm 45:1-8; 72:1-11)

7. What also was foretold of His relation to sin? (Isaiah 53; Zechariah 12:10)

8. What is the significance of the name which is applied to Christ? (John 1:29; Matthew 1:23)

9. What important facts are stated of Him in John 1:1-4?

A. _____

B. _____

C. _____

10. As part of the great scheme of human redemption, what did the Word become? What is the meaning of the words *"made flesh"*? (Matthew 1:23)

Notes

Geography Song

Oh, have you heard geography sung?
For if you've not, it's on my tongue;
About the earth in air that's hung,
     All covered with green little islands,
Oceans, gulfs, and bays, and seas,
Channels and straits, sounds if you please;
Great archipelagoes, too, and all these
     Are covered with green little islands.

All o'er the earth are water and land,
Beneath the ships, or where we stand;
And far beyond the ocean strand
     Are thousands of green little islands.
Continents and capes there are,
Isthmus and then peninsula,
Mountain and valley, and shore stretching far,
     And thousands of green little islands.

All o'er the globe some circles are found;
From east to west they stretch around;
Some go from north to southern bound,
     Right over the green little islands;
Great equator, tropics two,
Latitude lines, longitude too,
Cold polar circles, and all these go through
     The thousands of green little islands.

Oh! don't you think 'tis pleasant to know
About the sea and land just so,
And how the lines, the circles, go
     Right over the green little islands?
Now you hear how we can sing;
This is, today, all we can bring.
Come again soon, and you shall hear sung
     The names of the green little islands.
              —*Unknown*

Answer Key

Page 6

1. History is the footprints of events and people left in the sands of time. We can track these marks through periods of long ago and learn about the past.

2. Figurative = Something left behind that tells about a person, place, or an object or thing

Literal = A mark, outline or indentation left by a foot on a surface

3. See page 2.

4. Satan. The effect of his footprints was ruin.

5. The fact of the marks of sin and the fact of salvation.

6. History = An account of past events

Bible = God's history of this world and its people

Pages 10-11

Teacher, check.

Page 22

1. The world from way off in space looks something like a full moon— round and very bright.

2. A science that deals with the natural features of the earth and its climate, products, and inhabitants.

3. The past, the present, and the future.

4. Teacher, check.

5. It makes things pleasant and the people are able to develop in many ways to glorify God. (Answer can vary.)

6. The **love** of true Christianity.

7. See page 19.

8. Teacher, check. The child can use an encyclopedia.

9. Some homes have an atmosphere of **love** and pleasantness while others are "stormy" with harshness and unhappiness.

10. So that they can influence each other, make life more interesting and better, show contrast, etc.

Answer Key

Page 28

1. A foretelling of something to come.

Future events

2. Fulfilled prophecy.

3. Texts may vary: *"For the prophecy came not in old time by the will of man: but holy men of God spake as they were moved by the <u>Holy Ghost</u>"* (II Peter 1:21).

4. Christ's first coming and His second coming.

5. By beholding we become changed.

Page 63

1. The Lord Himself.

2. affected, mental, physical, providence, law

3. Parents were to teach their children God's requirements and to make them acquainted with all His dealings with their fathers. Thoughts of God were to be associated with all the events of daily life.

They were trained to see God alike in the scenes of nature and the words of revelation.

5. Further instruction could be obtained in the schools of the prophets.

Those who sought these schools were the pious, intelligent, and studious.

Samuel founded these schools to serve as a barrier against the widespread corruption, to provide for the moral and spiritual welfare of the youth, and to promote the future prosperity of the nation.

The students in these schools were called the sons of the prophets.

6. Two schools in Samuel's day and more later.

7. By their own labor.

Paul, Aquila, etc.

8. The law of God (Mathematics), with the instructions given to Moses, sacred history, sacred music, poetry, voice training, character development, nature, reading, health, and practical trades.

Answer Key

Page 63 continued

9. It was the grand object of all study to learn the will of God and man's duty toward Him. In the records of sacred history were traced the footsteps of Jehovah. The great truths set forth by the types were brought to view, and faith grasped the central object of all that system—the Lamb of God that was to take away the sin of the world.

10. See page 52.

11. Almost all of the modern institutions are governed by the maxims and customs of the world. (See page 53 for some examples.)

12. "The true object of education is to restore the image of God in the soul." (See page 53.)

Page 64

13. Teacher, check.

14. great, character building, knowledge, foundation, true.

15. To impart the above knowledge and to mold the character in harmony with it.

16. "It is a law of the mind that it gradually adapts itself to the subjects upon which it is trained to dwell. If occupied with commonplace matters only, it will become dwarfed and enfeebled." (See page 55.)

17. See page 56.

18. Brings fresh evidences of the wisdom and power of God.

19. That religion is not conducive to health or happiness in this life.

"The fear of the Lord tendeth to life: and he that hath it shall abide satisfied" (Proverbs 19:23). *"What man is he that desireth life, and loveth many days, that he may see good? Keep thy tongue from evil, and thy lips from speaking guile. Depart from evil, and do good; seek peace, and pursue it"* (Psalm 34:12-14). The words of wisdom *"are life unto those that find them, and health to all their flesh"* (Proverbs 4:22).

21. See page 59.

22. Teacher, check.

23. There is an intimate relation between the mind and the body, and

Answer Key

Page 64 continued

in order to reach a high standard of moral and intellectual attainment the laws that control our physical being must be heeded. To secure a strong, well-balanced character, both the mental and the physical powers must be exercised and developed.

24. Teacher, check.

25. Student answer.

Page 72

2. Some answers could be:

Abraham – James 2:23
Moses – Exodus 33:11
Elijah – II Kings 2:1

3. History = An account of past events

Geography = A science that deals with the natural features of the earth and its climate, products, and inhabitants

Prophecy = A foretelling of something to come

Notes

Music
for the Student Section

Gardening Sheet

Lesson ___One___   **Subject** ___H/G/P___

Title ___"What is H/G/P?"___

In Season

A well ordered garden shows the history of good pre-planning.

Good planning keeps flowers in sight of the house. Plan for some flowers in your vegetable garden. They add beauty to your vegetable garden, and also can keep some unwanted pests away by companion planting. They also attract beneficial insects. These flowers are like the flowers of history that bloom through the Bible—there is Abraham, Moses, Daniel, etc.; and Jesus the Flower of all flowers!

"I AM the rose of Sharon, and the lily of the valleys" (Song of Solomon 2:1).

Out of Season

Research and plan for flowers, and flowering shrubs that are perennials. Make a list. Find which ones grow best in your area. Draw them into your plan. Read the story about the flowers in *Steps to Christ*, pages 116-117.

Student
Section

"For the prophecy came not in old time
by the will of man:
but holy men of God spake
as they were moved by the holy Ghost."
II Peter 1:21

What is History?

Research
The Footprints of God

"And, Thou, Lord, in the beginning hast laid the foundation of the earth; and the heavens are the works of thine hands."

Hebrews 1:10

History is the footprints of events and people left in the sands of time. We can track these marks through periods of long ago and learn about the past.

The story is told about an Arab. When someone came to him in his tent in the desert, and said to him, "How do you know there is a God?" He said, "How do I know whether it was a man or a camel that went by my tent last night?" How did he know which it was? "By the footprints." The marks in the sand showed whether it was a man's foot or a camel's foot that had passed his tent. So the Arab said, "That is the way I know God. I know Him by His footprints. There are His footprints that are all around me."

Literal
Footprint = A mark, outline or indentation left by a foot on a surface.

Figurative
Footprint = Something left behind that tells about a person, place, or an object or thing.

History = An account of past events.

Bible = God's history of this world and its people.

In the first chapter of the Bible, figuratively speaking, we can see how God left His footprints in the creation of this earth.

History
deals with the past.

"In the beginning God created the heaven and the earth" (Genesis 1:1). On the **first** day, God made *"light;"* on the **second** day, *"the firmament;"* on the **third** day, *"waters gathered, dry land, grass, the herb, and trees;"* on the **fourth** day, *"sun, moon, and stars;"* on the **fifth** day, *"moving creatures in the water, fowls, and birds;"* and on the **sixth** day, *"living creatures, cattle, creeping things, beasts, and man."* Did the greatest thing come first or last? Did it always go on improving? What sort of life did God make first? He made plants; then animal life, then what was next? Human life. A being that could **love** and worship Him.

God never made anything till He had first made or immediately after what it needed to live. Plants needed soil, sunshine, and water to live. Sea creatures needed water and food, while birds needed air and food and trees for building their nests. Land animals needed homes, water, and food. Man would need a place to live, food to eat, water to drink, clothing, and creative things to do to expand his mind.

Remember that all through life, God allows circumstances that He has also provided power for man that he will need, to be **loving**, happy and productive for God.

God made man a home for we are told: *"And the LORD God took the man and put him into the garden of Eden, to dress it and to keep it"* (Genesis 2:15).

Imagine the first man and woman as they stand in the midst of flowers and great palm trees, with the birds flitting around them, and animals laying at their feet.

When a painter has painted a beautiful picture, he does not make a frame for it with four rough, ugly sticks. If the picture is the best he has painted, he puts the best frame around it. And if a man has a beautiful diamond, he does not encase it with a bit of old iron; he fashions a beautiful gold clasp for it. The best always deserves to be set in the choice setting. And so, since the crowning jewels, of God's creation were so perfect, He placed Adam and Eve in the magnificent Garden of Eden, prepared by God, Himself. It was a little bit of heaven brought to earth.

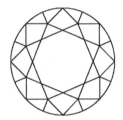 

However, **lovely** the surroundings, they do not always make **lovely** hearts. The third chapter of Genesis describes the most beautiful place, the most perfect pair, and the saddest home-leaving in the world.

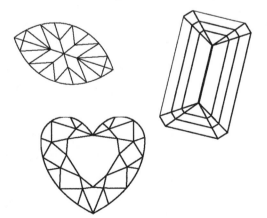

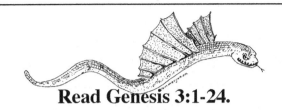

Read Genesis 3:1-24.

Satan sinned and was cast out of the Eden of heaven and came to this world to leave a different kind of footprint on it.

Many a child, hearing the story of Adam's and Eve's fall have asked, "Mother, why did God not keep the serpent out of the garden? Isn't God stronger than anyone, and couldn't He have kept Satan out if He had liked?" Were a father to shut up his son in a room for life, and not allow him to see any one, that boy would be kept from many wrongs into which friends would fall. But he would never develop his character as God planned for him. If he is ever to be a godly man, he must have scope and liberty with all its risks. Thus God left the angels and Adam and Eve free to make their choices. Again, it may seem hard that so small a sin should bring so great a curse. But was it a small sin? The sin of the hand seemed small—stealing a piece of fruit; but the sin of the heart was great; for it rebelled against God, broke His law, and scorned Him. The stealing of $1.00 makes a man a thief quite as much as the stealing of $1,000.00. Every sin is great that dishonors the Creator.

A man was once carrying a splendid jewel to the king, when he was seized by robbers who knew what he had in his pocket. He offered them his purse, his rings, his horse, his clothes, but they only laughed and said, "We will take the diamond and those things too." So the Devil—that great Robber—is determined to have your purity, kindness, joyfulness, and **love** for God. If it is saved, all is saved; if it be lost, all is lost.

One of the great sights at the Exhibition in London in 1851 was the Kohinoor diamond. It was kept inside a glass case, within another glass case, in a small tent, and an armed soldier guarded it. It was preserved so carefully, because it was worth so much money. But, your soul—who can give a name to its value? It is worth more than all the gold, silver, and jewels in the whole world. By faith and prayer commit it unto God's safe keeping; and then you will be *"hid with Christ in God,"* like a jewel well guarded. None shall be able to pluck you out of the Father's hand.

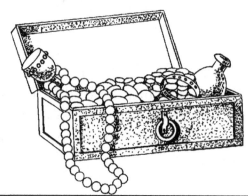

After the fall there is only one word to describe what happened—*Ruin.* God promised Adam and Eve and their descendants His help. *"And I will put enmity between thee and the woman, and between thy seed and her seed; it shall bruise thy head, and thou shalt bruise his heel"* (Genesis 3:15). He then drove them out of the beautiful Garden of Eden. He placed cherubim with a flaming sword which turned every way, to keep or guard the way of the tree of life.

The curse did not stop there; it had changed everything on this earth. Satan left his evil footprints on God's perfect world. The flowers died, weeds grow, trees were deformed, plants became poisonous, animals were ferocious, the air became tainted, the sun scorched people, and the water became impure.

As the earth turns upon two poles, so the Bible turns upon the two great facts—the fact of the marks of sin and the fact of salvation.

We are told in our Bible lesson, "In the beginning, God was revealed in all the works of creation. ...Now sin [Satan's footprints] has marred God's perfect work, yet that handwriting [God's footprints] remains...No bird that cleaves the air, no animal that moves upon the ground, but ministers to some other life. There is no leaf of the forest, or lowly blade of grass, but has its ministry. Every tree and shrub and leaf pours forth that element of life without which neither man nor animal could live; and man and animal, in turn minister to the life of tree and shrub and leaf. The flowers breathe fragrance and unfold their beauty in blessing to the world. The sun sheds its light to gladden a thousand worlds. The ocean, itself the source of all our springs and fountains, receives the streams from every land, but takes to give. The mists ascending from its bosom fall in showers to water the earth, that it may bring forth and bud....

"But turning from all lesser representations, we behold God in Jesus. Looking unto Jesus we see that it is the glory of God to give...."*

"By coming to dwell with us, Jesus was to reveal God both to men and to angels."** He was to show the **love** of God in the footprints He left behind. Mathew, Mark, Luke, John, and *The Desire of Ages* are books full of His footsteps.

In Bible history we will follow a few of these tracks through books which will show us how God leads His people in the narrow path.

History could be made into two words, "His story." In History we will learn the story of the **love** of Christ for His people as He created them and then came to dwell among them.

It is important for us to diligently study the history of the Bible. The following text explains why. *"Now all these things happened unto them for ensamples: and they are written for our admonition, upon whom the ends of the world are come"* (I Corinthians 10:11).

Read the story, "Their Treasure."

*The Desire of Ages 20-21   **The Desire of Ages 19

Review
Place I – II – III

1. What thoughts can footprints bring to our minds? Why?

2. Give the definition of the figurative and literal meaning of the word "footprint."

3. Describe how God left His footprints in creation.

4. Who else left footprints and how did it affect this earth?

5. What two facts does the Bible turn upon?

6. Define the words history and Bible.

Reinforce

1. Find tracks of an animal and try to follow its path. Remember the school lesson by considering God's path when He came from heaven to walk on this earth for over 33 years.

2. Make your footprint in soft soil. Share with your teacher the kind of history you would like to leave behind as you walk through life.

3. Trace your footprint, then copy your memory verses on them. Share these footprints with family members or friends.

4. Do you know your family history? Talk with older family members to discover it.

Remind

1. When taking your shoes off at night, look at the soles of your feet, think about God's footsteps on this earth.

2. Snakes can remind you of Satan's footprints on this world. What kind of prints on the ground do snakes make?

3. As you use your Bible daily, you can call it your spiritual history book.

Learn about animal tracks and how to follow them.

Their Treasure

"Thy word is a lamp unto my feet, and a light unto my path."
Psalm 119:105

"Wife, we cannot leave this book behind," said the man, as he came from the little Armenian church. "It is heavy, and if I take it, something else must be left. But this must go with us. It is too precious to lose, and we shall need it." As he spoke, he laid aside one of the things that he had intended to take on their flight to safety, and put the pulpit Bible in its place.

It was during the massacres of 1909 in Turkey and Syria, and a whole village, having heard that the Turks were coming, was hurriedly leaving the valley. Men, women, and children; animals, bedding, and cooking utensils; food and furniture- it was a motley array of things that go to make up a home. Soon the line reached far out toward the mountain over which they must go. All of the men were loaded with things; most of the women carried children, and among the rest walked the church deacon with the Bible which had been given to their church by Dr. Elias Riggs in memory of his daughter. It had first been a gift of the father to his daughter on her fiftieth wedding anniversary, so it was a very fine book. It was one of the treasures in the village, and the Christians had been proud to have it in their church.

At first the bundles did not seem to be very heavy, as the exiles hurried on, but as the way grew steeper, articles began to be abandoned. As long as he could find strength to do so, the man carried the Bible, but at last, from sheer weariness, he placed it tenderly on a stone near the road, gave it a last loving look, and went on his tedious way. All were too heavily loaded to help him; night was coming, and he must hurry along. Strangely enough, no one seemed to notice that the Bible had been left behind.

After darkness had settled over the path, a woman came along, carrying one little child and dragging another after her. She had been left behind because she could not keep up with the rest.

"I must rest," she said at last. "I can go no farther." As she started to sit down on a rock by the road, her hand struck something unfamiliar. She felt of it and turned it over. "It is a book," she said. "I believe it is our church Bible. Who could have left it here? That is too precious to leave. Somehow I must take it."

A half hour later, when she wearily rose to her feet, she left behind the extra blanket which she had brought for the protection of the children and took the Bible. When she finally came to the next village, she found that the enemy were already there and that the women had all taken refuge in an old Gregorian church for the night. About the streets was an ugly, fighting crowd of men and boys. She crept cautiously to the door of the church and whispered her name. It opened a very little and she went inside. On the floor were several hundred women and children, huddled together, their faces full of terror, hardly daring to speak above a whisper.

The woman came to them lovingly and whispered: "Don't worry, neighbors. I have our Bible." One whispered it to another, "She has our Bible," until the whole room had heard the good news.

"I have a little candle that I found near the door," said some one in a hushed voice.

"And I have one match," whispered another.

The woman carried her Bible into the center of the group and sat down. She lighted the one little candle with the one lone match, while the women shaded it with their clothing lest its flame be seen outside the church. Then in the darkness of the church there came to be felt a new Presence as she read from the Word:

" *Thou shalt not be afraid of the terror by night, nor for the arrow that flieth by day. A thousand shall fall at thy side, and ten thousand at thy right hand, but it shall not come nigh thee. For he shall give his angels charge over thee to keep thee in all thy ways.'* " On and on, she read the promises of God.

When the candle had burned itself out they were less afraid and they could still feel the presence of the Book in their midst. So they quoted to each other the verses which they had learned from the Book in their own little church until they fell asleep there on the floor of the old church.

For two days and two nights they stayed there, expecting every moment that the doors would be broken in; but when they went out they were safe, for the enemy had gone.

"It was very strange," said a man to one of the women later in the week. "The enemy tried again and again to burn the church. They even tried to pour kerosene through the roof and burn you, but something seemed to hold them back. Every effort seemed to fail. I do not understand at all."

But the woman did. *"God is a refuge and strength; a very present help in trouble."* The Book said so.

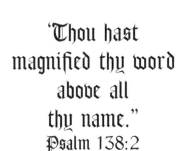

'Thou hast
magnified thy word
above all
thy name."
Psalm 138:2

'The grass withereth,
the flower fadeth:
but the word of our God
shall stand for ever."
Isaiah 40:8

Reflect
The Bible
is the Best History Book.

When studying history it is not good to let our minds dwell upon evil deeds and people, names of people we do not need to know, and meaningless dates.

Remember God's word... *"The sinners in Zion are afraid; fearfulness hath surprised the hypocrites. Who among us shall dwell with the devouring fire? who among us shall dwell with everlasting burnings?*

"He that walketh righteously, and speaketh uprightly; he that despiseth the gain of oppressions, that shaketh his hands from holding of bribes, <u>that stoppeth his ears from hearing of blood, and shutteth his eyes from seeing evil</u>" (Isaiah 33:14-15).

What is Love?

"Let brotherly love continue."
Hebrews 13:1

Our little world could be called a history book for the rest of the universe. It is a volume that will be studied throughout eternity. The theme of this record is Jesus giving tireless **love** to His creation.

Christ came to earth and has thrown His great arms of **love** around the human race. He has brought His divine power to man that He might encourage them to walk in His way. If we follow in Christ's footsteps, we then demonstrate His life, His **love**, and show it to those around us.

> Keep your feet in the <u>footprints</u> of Christ.
> He said, *"Follow Me."*

God describes what **love** is in I Corinthians 13:1-8, 13. <u>After each verse write what it is saying to you. Use the *Strong's Concordance* to define the words you do not understand.</u>

This activity is for **Place II - III**. Ask your teacher for help.

The Bible says: 1 *"Though I speak with the tongues of men and of angels, and have not* **charity***, I am become as sounding brass, or a tinkling cymbal.*

———————————————
———————————————
———————————————

2 *"And though I have the gift of prophecy, and understand all mysteries, and all knowledge; and though I have all faith, so that I could remove mountains, and have not* **charity***, I am nothing.*

———————————————
———————————————
———————————————

3 *"And though I bestow all my goods to feed the poor, and though I give my body to be burned, and have not* **charity***, it profiteth me nothing.*

———————————————
———————————————

4 *"***Charity*** suffereth long, and is kind;* **charity** *envieth not;* **charity** *vaunteth not itself, is not puffed up,*

———————————————
———————————————
———————————————

> Sing the hymn,
> "Follow All the Way."

5 *"Doth not behave itself unseemly, seeketh not her own, is not easily provoked, thinketh no evil;*

_____

_____

_____

6 *"Rejoiceth not in iniquity, but rejoiceth in the truth;*

_____

_____

_____

7 *"Beareth all things, believeth all things, hopeth all things, endureth all things.*

_____

_____

_____

8 *"**Charity** never faileth: but whether there be prophecies, they shall fail; whether there be tongues, they shall cease; whether there be knowledge, it shall vanish away.*

_____

_____

_____

9 *"For we know in part, and we prophesy in part.*

_____

_____

_____

10 *"But when that which is perfect is come, then that which is in part shall be done away.*

_____

_____

11 *"When I was a child, I spake as a child, I understood as a child, I thought as a child: but when I became a man, I put away childish things.*

_____

_____

_____

12 *"For now we see through a glass, darkly; but then face to face: now I know in part; but then shall I know even as also I am known.*

_____

_____

_____

13 *"And Now abideth faith, hope, **charity**, these three; but the greatest of these is **charity**."*

_____

_____

Love

Reflect

Love = An affection of the mind which God has excited by showing beauty and worth of an individual; then serving the person; charity.

'Herein is love,
not that we <u>loved</u> God,
but that he <u>loved</u> us,
and sent his Son
to be the propitiation
for our sins.

'Beloved
if God so <u>loved</u> us,
we ought also
to <u>love</u> one another."

I John 4:10-11

In the books of John, it says *"God is light"* (I John 1:5) and *"God is love"* (I John 4:8). Light is energy that flows over the whole earth to all people without discrimination. His **love** is a quality that is freely given to all. *"But as many as received him, to them gave he power to become the sons of God, even to them that believe on his name"* (John 1:12).

God's Love

In every plant and flower
  God's power and **love** we see;
But greater far, He sent His Son
  To die for you and me.

Oh, shall not we accept
  This **love** so freely given,
And daily walk with Him on earth,
  And reign with Him in heaven?

—Paulina M.A. Anderson

Loving People Whom We Do Not Like

"He that <u>loveth</u> his brother
abideth in the light,
and there is none occasion
of stumbling in him."
1 John 2:10

This world is full of various kinds of people. It would be a very monotonous world if it were not. It is the variety which gives it interest. But many of these different sorts of people do not feel kindly toward other sorts. "We are not congenial," they say. "I simply cannot endure that girl," one girl says of another. "Her taste in dress is outrageous, and her giggling and general silliness are intolerable." The other girl says, "I do not like that precise person, who never acts naturally nor forgets primness." And there are deeper dislikes than these.

Now, many of these dislikes we can not help—at first; but they have nothing to do with **loving**. **Loving** and liking are different things. Jesus did not say, *"A new commandment I give unto you, That ye like one another;"* but, *"A new commandment I give unto you, That ye **love** one another."* **Love** rises above like, and can exist in spite of dislike.

We like what pleases us. We **love** what we would please. Liking is selfish. **Loving** is unselfish. Liking depends on its object; **loving** upon its subject. If the person we like changes, we may dislike him, but no change in the person **loved** can alter **love**. Even at the best, liking is a feeble thing, capricious [large, expansive, widespread], unreliable; but **loving** is deep and eternal. It is good enough to speak of liking things, but whether we like persons or not is a matter of small consequence. The real question is, Do we **love** them?*

*M. C. Hazard

"Mother, I Must Speak!"

A business meeting was being held in a certain place, and the tempers ran very high. Those present accused one another and justified themselves in a quite unbecoming manner. There were present in the meeting a Christian lady and her little daughter, a child of some five years, who had been brought up in a Christian home.

As the meeting continued, and charges and counter-charges were made by the contending parties, this little girl grew restless, and turned to her mother, and whispered, "Mother, I must speak!" The parent immediately hushed the child; and told her it was no place for her to speak, and that she must be very still. On this the child quieted down, while the accusing element in the meeting seemed to rise higher and yet higher.

Shortly the child turned again to her mother as if to rise to her feet, while she repeated her request with greater emphasis, saying, "Mother, I must speak!" The mother, now in a very decided manner, told her that she must keep quiet; that this meeting was no place for a little girl like her to say anything. And so for the second time she was compelled to remain silent.

But the wrong spirit that ruled in the house had full sway, and there was no little excitement and confusion. The child now for the third time pulled her mother's arm, and with greater earnestness than before urged her request, saying, "MOTHER, I MUST SPEAK!"

The mother, now feeling that the Spirit of the Lord was moving on the child, dared object no longer, and she answered by saying, "Well, you may speak."

The little girl immediately arose to her feet, and spreading out her hands, as if entreating those present, said, in a clear voice, *"Let brotherly love continue,"* and then at once sat down.

The result of this little speech was like suddenly turning on a number of electric lights in a dark room. The meeting immediately broke up, and the contending elements left the house reproved and ashamed. All felt that they had seen a beautiful fulfillment of the Scripture, *"And a little child shall lead them."*

What is Geography?

Research
Our World

"He hath made the earth by his power,
he hath established the world by his wisdom...."
Jeremiah 10:12

Very few people have ever seen our own world—the planet Earth—all at one time.

You can see a little bit of the world around you—and if you go up into a high building you can see more—and if you go up into a high mountain you can see more—and if you go up in an airplane you can even see more.

But to see the whole world you would have to go much higher than buildings, mountains, or airplanes. You would have to go up in a spacecraft—very high above this planet.

If you lived on an island surrounded by water, it would seem the earth was made up of water.

However, if you lived in the desert it would look like it was a huge pile of sand.

But if you lived in the mountains it would appear like a large forest with lots and lots of trees.

Geography
deals with the past,
the present, and the future.

Geography = A science that deals with the natural features of the earth and its climate, products, and inhabitants.

If you were in the jungle—it would be thick foliage and noisy wildlife everywhere.

Perhaps you have visited a very cold place like Alaska where it looks like ice and snow could dominate the whole earth.

As you grow and mature, you realize that the world is like a big mud pie with some water, some sand, some mountains, some trees and foliage, and some snow and ice.

The world is just a big island spinning through space and this is what you call home.

The world from way off in space looks something like a full moon—round and very bright—for the sun shines on this big ball, our world, Earth, and makes it light just as the headlights on an automobile shine on the road at night and make the road light. Of course, the sun can shine on only one side of this big ball at a time; the other side of the world is dark, but the world keeps turning round and round in the sunlight.

If you looked at the world through a telescope, as men look at the moon, you would see on one side of the world two big patches that look like shadows; and on the other side of the world, four shadows. These shadows are land and are called continents. The continents have names: North America, South America, Europe, Asia, Africa, Australia, and Antarctica.

We call one side of the world the western hemisphere and the other side the eastern hemisphere. Hemisphere means "half a ball." The western hemisphere has two continents and the eastern hemisphere has four continents. Antarctica is in both hemispheres.

The very top and the very bottom of the world are called the poles. Around the top and bottom pole it is white, for the poles are so cold that there is snow and ice there all the time.

The part of the world that is not land is water. The water all around the continents is the ocean, and its different parts are called by different names.

The Atlantic Ocean is on the east side of North and South America. The Pacific Ocean is on the west. The ocean entirely in the eastern hemisphere is called the Indian Ocean. At the top of the world is the Arctic Ocean. At the bottom, all around Antarctica, is the Antarctic Ocean. The Arctic and Antarctic Oceans are mostly ice, for it is so cold there the water freezes and stays frozen.

You may wonder, "Are there any other worlds besides ours?"

Hebrews 1:1-2, and 11:3 says: *"God...Hath in these last days spoken unto us by his Son, whom he hath appointed heir of all things, by whom also he made the <u>worlds</u>."*

"Through faith we understand that the <u>worlds</u> were framed by the word of God, so that things which are seen were not made of things which do appear."

Illustration
Hemispheres

Western Hemisphere

Eastern Hemisphere

As you study the people who live on this planet, you will want to know more about them and their surroundings. Geography can be taught with the past (History), the present (History in the making), or the future (Prophecy). There are six continents where people have lived in the past and present. In the future when God recreates the earth it will be very different then it is today.

Remember, geography is the study of the natural features of the earth—its climate, products, and inhabitants. In studying geography the one key point to keep in mind is, "How can you help those people from home and abroad to learn about the true story of the **love** of Christ, His first coming, and soon, His second coming? What are their needs? What mission work—on each continent—is going on? How can I find names and addresses for these mission stations that I might correspond with them?" Talk with your local church pastor or godly friends and you will find adequate places to serve by sharing what God has given you.

How can you help those people from other countries to learn about the true story of the <u>love</u> of Christ, His first coming, and soon, His second coming?

Surroundings and Atmosphere

"But we all, with open face beholding as in a glass the glory of the Lord, are changed into the same image from glory to glory, even as by the Spirit of the Lord."
II Corinthians 3:18

Did you know mankind is affected by his surroundings—by the way they look and by their atmosphere? It is a spiritual law that by beholding we become changed. (See II Corinthians 3:18.) We human beings are so closely connected with the world of nature around us that its mountains, valleys, deserts, seas and climate exercise a power over us that enters into our mental and moral character. God's *"hands formed the dry land"* and indirectly He molds us by our environment (Psalm 95:5). One illustration of this relationship between the land and character would be the way that people who live in lush, tropical climates usually tend to be easygoing in their outlook on life. They naturally do not develop in the same ways that people in harsher climates do because there is not so much of a need to work hard to produce food or survive, generally speaking.

God has made the different countries of the world to look different so that as people living in them behold the peculiar beauties of their country, and as they are compelled to deal with the problems associated with each climate, their characters develop in unique ways that reveal the many aspects of God's image. Thus the geography of each continent influences its history and even, to some extent, its place in prophecy.

It is just the same with us in our homes. Each home has a different atmosphere. The social "climate" varies with the dispositions of the people living under the same roof. Where there is **love**, the climate is pleasant and the people are able to develop in many ways that glorify God. But even in those homes that have a stormy or harsh atmosphere, people can learn to adapt to the situation. They can witness to God's sustaining grace in a way that others in more favorable circumstances cannot. *"Thou wilt keep him in perfect peace, whose mind is stayed on thee; because he trusteth in thee"* (Isaiah 26:3).

God can mold us by our environment.

The great seas of the world divide the land masses of the earth. In the peculiar arrangements of land and water on the surface of the earth, we have plain evidence of God's purpose of separating mankind into different nationalities. The Biblical story of the tower of Babel also assures us that this is God's intention. God saw that it would not be good for mankind to be permitted to remain indefinitely in one region of the earth. Being in close and constant communion with each other would have led to the growth of great evil because of the state of most of mankind's heart. We have only to look at the crime rate in our cities today to see this problem. People lose their sensitivity to evil when they live in close contact with it. God therefore separated mankind, placing them, over a period of time, in different scenes and circumstances as He saw best for them. As a result, different national characters were formed. Human nature has been modified throughout history into countless variations by the force of the different circumstances in which men live.

It was once said that "as the individuality of each man is that peculiar influence with which he is entrusted for the good of society, so the individuality of nations is that peculiar influence with which they are entrusted for the benefit of the world." If men were not individuals with different qualities, they would not be able to influence each other. How boring it would be if we were all alike. We would lose the sense of contrast and with it the feeling of personality. As far as the continents and nations of the earth go, if there was no individuality among them, mankind would not progress very much. We could not learn how to do many things better; having lost the benefit of each other's experience and instruction. The advances of one nation stimulate other nations to improve. The problems solved on one continent serve as an example to help others.

God wanted the **love** of true Christianity to form a spiritual connecting link between the continents. The gospel of Christ is designed to bring all mankind into contact for the **loving** purpose of sharing all the helpful excellencies which have been developed in their separate lands. Through this means they were to enrich each other by stores of knowledge and experience and spiritual insights which each had accumulated apart. This is why God situated the Jewish nation where He did at the crossroads of the world. But, sad to say, they failed in sharing God's **love** with other nations. The Jews had infinite advantages over the other countries of the world *"because that unto them were committed the oracles of God"* (Romans 3:2). God's word that told them how to excel in everything needful for this life. (See II Peter 1:3.) These things were committed to them as a sacred trust just as they are to us today. Will we be more faithful in sharing them is the question.

The Bible tells us that until the end of the earth there will be nations, and kindreds and tongues and peoples. (See Revelation 14:6.) But on the earth made new John saw that *"there was no more sea"* (Revelation 21:1). At that time there will be no need for separating oceans to serve as a check on the growth of evil *"for the iniquity of Israel shall be sought for; and there shall be none; and the sins of Judah, and they shall not be found"* (Jeremiah 50:20).

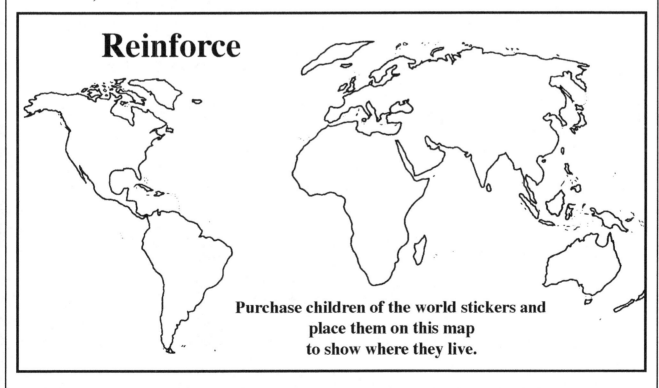

Reinforce

Purchase children of the world stickers and place them on this map to show where they live.

Review

Place I - II - III

1. Describe this earth as the universe sees it.

2. Define geography.

3. What element of time does geography deal with?

4. Give an example of geography in the past, present, and future.

5. How does **love** affect the climate of a home?

6. What can be the connecting link between continents?

Place II - III

7. How is man affected by his environment?

8. **Thought Question**: How does the people and climate of _____ differ from _____? (Choose two countries and compare.)

9. Explain how homes have different atmospheres.

10. Why is it important for man and woman and children to be individuals?

Reinforce

1. Find a picture of people from each of the six continents and notice the difference and similarities about them.

2. Make a list of the things that affect your environment.

3. Go for a nature walk and note to your teacher things you can see from the past, present, and what may be different in the future. (Example: Past—mountains; present—garden; and future—plans for a rock garden.)

4. Read the story, "Forgotten People."

Remind

1. Notice how when someone smiles at you that it is very hard not to smile back. It can remind you how we are changed by beholding our surroundings.

2. Choose something that is special to your area that affects the people around there.

Forgotten People

"Give and it shall be given unto you...."
Luke 6:38

**Jesus came to dwell with man
to demonstrate His <u>love</u> by giving His life.
As you read this story
think about people in other countries and their needs.**

There was a student-preacher in a village in Texas. The Christmas season was approaching and members of his congregation decided to present the story of the first Christmas in Bethlehem. His ingenuity and tact were taxed to the limit. Everybody, it seemed, wanted to be a part of this program.

At last some sort of harmony was established and for the program began. Just then a poor family of wandering people camped on the outskirts of the village. They were nearly destitute; several of them were quite ill; yet nobody seemed to pay any attention to them. Those from whom they might have expected assistance were too busy preparing to present a pageant of something which happened many centuries ago to bother with present-day wretchedness. Afterward it was discovered that the only good Samaritan in the village was an old bachelor living in a shack, an old fellow considered by most to be more or less of a ne'er-do-well. He took soup and other foodstuffs to the unfortunates and nursed them in their sickness while others went on with their preparations.

One day Jesus visited the pool of Bethesda not far from the temple in Jerusalem. There He saw a poor paralytic who had lain by the pool for twenty-eight years. That is a long time for people who are well; how much longer it must have seemed to that weary cripple! Some passed him hundreds of times—so often that they ceased to know he was there. He was friendless, lonely, discouraged; no one paid any attention to him. One commentator suggests that he might even have heard the sound of worship from the temple. In that building the priests made sure to keep the fire burning on the altar. It must never go out, but no one thought it worth while to keep the fires of hope burning in the heart of that forgotten sufferer by the side of the pool. To Jesus he said: *"Sir, I have no man, when the water is troubled, to put me into the pool."*

In Old Mortality, Scott told of an old man who wandered over the heather-covered hills and lonely moors of Scotland seeking out the graves of the martyred Covenanters. Sometimes he found the stones which marked their resting places covered with moss and fretted with decay. With his knife he scraped away the fungus and then, taking his chisel, labored with loving touch until he had made the name stand out clear and distinct. He had little interest in the things for which other men longed and fought, but keeping alive the memory of brave men—for this he lived. If he could help it, they would not be forgotten.

It is well to remember the lives of holy people; to forget them would be unpardonable ingratitude, but we should not forget the living. There are everywhere people who have been forgotten, those who are taken for granted and dismissed from consideration as was this paralytic. They have long been with us and appear to have little place in the scheme of things. We are so busy with the complex machinery of life that, like the people with their Christmas program or the priests keeping alive the fires on the temple altar, we overlook the duty near at hand.

Someday we may be humiliated to find how utterly lacking in imagination we ourselves have been. These charming little verses by Elizabeth Coatsworth express regrets which many of us may feel:

To think I once saw grocery shops
With but a casual eye,
And fingered figs and apricots
As one who came to buy.

To think I never dreamed of how
Bananas sway in rain,
And often looked at oranges
And never thought of Spain.

And in those wasted days I saw
No sails above the tea
For grocery shops were grocery shops,
Not hemispheres to me.

A gentleman once visited a man nearing the end of his journey here who had some grounds for complaint. Many years previously he had been a church member. Trouble arose in the congregation and in a fit of anger the man withdrew and declared he would never attend any church again. Urgent invitations to reconsider his stand only increased his stubbornness. After a while his friends in the church and community accepted his position and ceased even to show concern over his spiritual condition. Meanwhile the man began to regret his hasty words and his vow. The death of his wife and later of a child found him longing for sympathy and for the peace the church had brought him in happier days.

But no one thought—or ventured—to speak to him of such things. By this time his antipathy to church was taken for granted and, as with the man by the side of the Bethesda pool, there was no one at the right moment to come to his assistance. He talked of these incidents in the closing hours of his life without bitterness but not without regret; in his own mind there was some sense of wonder that he had been so completely passed by.

In his letter to the Colossians, Paul talked of the responsibility the Church had *"toward them that are without."* All over the country earnest ministers and devoted laymen have shown commendable zeal in seeking to attract outsiders. Some of the methods adopted may not always be the wisest or in good taste, but the solemn sense of responsibility is in itself a good thing. Christians know and must believe that of all that happens to people here on earth nothing is so vital and important as their spiritual condition. The business of the church is to seek the outsiders and to do it with something of the Lord's passion. These lines voice what we must all feel:

Be swift, dear heart, in **loving**,
For time is brief,
And thou mayest soon along life's highway
Keep step with grief.

Be swift, dear heart, in saying
The kindly word.
When ears are sealed, thy passionate
                                    pleading
Will not be heard.

Be swift, dear heart, in doing
The gracious deed.
Lest soon they whom thou holdest dearest
Be past the need.

Dear heart, be swift in **loving**.
Time speedeth on.
And all thy chance of blessed service
Will soon be gone.

Prayer: "Father, we have often been distressed because men and women have been indifferent to the sorrows of others. Their failures have grieved us, yet we ourselves have been negligent and complacent. Lord forbid that we should live in the past, ignoring the duties and the privileges near at hand. Open our eyes lest we be blind and deaf to those who need us. Amen."

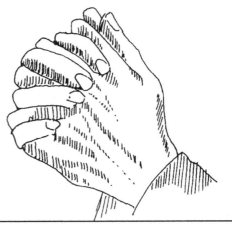

What is Prophecy?

Research
Future Events

"For the prophecy came not in old time by the will of man: but holy men of God spake as they were moved by the Holy Ghost."
II Peter 1:21

"Prophecy is history revealed in advance. To the prophets were revealed future events which had to do with individuals and with nations. With God, a thousand years are but as yesterday and as a watch in the night (Psalm 90:4). He knows the end from the beginning (Isaiah 46:9-10). He mentioned by name Cyrus, a king of Persia, nearly two hundred years before his birth, and fortold the capture of Babylon, and the means employed to accomplish the seemingly impossible task.

"The rise of nations, their character and destiny, have been revealed through the prophets. These prophecies were studied in the Hebrew school, and should be studied with their fulfillment in the school of today.

"Fulfilled prophecy is the strongest testimony that can be produced confirming the inspiration of the Bible. Accordingly the sacred Scriptures and secular history will be studied hand in hand. The latter is the record of human life, and the former is necessary to its right interpretation."*

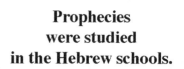

Prophecies were studied in the Hebrew schools.

Prophecy deals with <u>the future</u>.

Prophecy = A foretelling of something to come. As God only knows future events with certainty, no being but God or some person informed by Him, can utter a real prophecy.

Adapted from The Education That Educates 161-162

Important Prophecies

"For the Son of man shall come in the glory of his Father with his angels; and then he shall reward every man according to his works."
Matthew 16:27

In God's word many important prophecies are given. Two of the most important were Christ's first coming and His second coming. In **love** God tried to prepare the Hebrew people for the event of His first coming. They were not prepared. In **love** today He wants us to be ready for His Second Coming. Will He have a people ready? Yes! Will you be one of them?

Later in this course you will study the great prophecies that tell us Christ is coming soon. We also will learn more about the United States as relating to prophecy.

Reflect

"So likewise ye, when ye shall see all these things, know that it is near, even at the doors."
Matthew 24:33

The Cycle of a Nation

1. Bondage – captivity, slavery.

2. Spiritual Faith – turning to God.

3. Acts of Great Courage – doing what is right despite difficulty, danger, pain.

4. Liberty and Abundance – freedom and great blessings.

5. Selfishness – regard for one's own interest (at other's expense).

6. Complacency – quiet satisfaction.

7. Apathy – indifference, lack of emotion.

8. Dependency – control or influence by another.

9. Bondage – captivity, slavery.
Source Unknown

Review
Place I - II - III

1. What does the word prophecy mean? What is another word for prophecy?

2. What is the strongest testimony to confirm the inspiration of the Bible?

3. Where does prophecy come from? Answer with a Bible text.

4. What are the two most important prophecies given in Scripture?

5. Why is it not good to dwell upon evil deeds and people?

Reinforce

1. Ask an older person what life was like when they were a child. (Past)

2. Compare what they said about the way life was then as to what it is today. (Present)

3. Read in the Bible prophecy of what life will be like in the future. (Either on the new earth or during the time of trouble.)

Take notes by writing down what you have learned.

4. Read the poem, "The Sure Word of Prophecy."

5. Read the story, "William Miller."

The Sure Word of Prophecy

The sure prophetic light
      Is shining on the way;
To lead us safe through Time's dark night,
      Till dawns the endless day.
The Word, the track has laid,
      And all the way-marks given,
Each station marked along the grade,
      Till saints arrive at heaven.

The Engine, Providence,
      Has sped adown this track,
Has made each station once, and thence
      It never has rolled back.
No "baggage" is attached,
      To please the grasping mind:
But all who are from ruin snatched,
      Must leave it all behind.

Salvation's car propelled
      By power of Heavenly **Love**,
From age to age its course has held,
      To bear the saints above.
The saints in every age,
      Who trials have endured,
And borne earth's scoffs and Satan's rage,
      A passage have secured.

The Train has reached the place,
      The last upon the road,
Where any soul of all our race,
      May hope to get aboard.
O, let us not delay
      A passage to secure;
Let us not rest a single day,
      Until we make it sure.

William Miller

*"For whatsoever things were written aforetime
were written for our learning,
that we through patience and comfort of the scriptures
might have hope."*
Romans 15:4

Converted Infidel and Baptist Evangelist
Born at Pittsfield, Massachusetts, February 15, 1782.
Died at Low Hampton, New York, December 20, 1849.

How different are God's ways from man's! At a time when French infidelity was running riot in the land of God's providence, whom should He select but one who was for years an avowed deist, to hurl such polished shafts from His mighty quiver against the citadel of the adversary, that its very foundations trembled—six thousand conversions resulting from the labors of this one man, seven hundred infidels being won by him to the faith of Christ!

When we consider that such amazing inroads upon gospel-hardened infidelity were probably made by no other individual in the past century, and that this was accomplished in a campaign of less than twenty years, it is apparent that a higher than human hand was in the movement; and to enter into a sympathetic acquaintance with the labors of William Miller is to enrich greatly one's spiritual life.

In the year that gave Robert Morrison to the world, William Miller was born. The library to which the thoughtful boy had access for some years was the Bible, the psalter, and a prayer-book. On the removal of the family to Low Hampton, New York, he obtained other books, and wished to spend his evenings studying; but the father insisted on his retiring early. This he did; but after all were asleep, he would get up, put pine knots into the fireplace, and read by their glimmering light. "The most embarrassing circumstances of his condition," says his biographer, Mr. Bliss, "could not master his perseverance."

He was happily married in 1803, and settled in Vermont. His wife made it her pleasure to aid his efforts for intellectual training. His sterling enterprise and integrity gained for him a competence in temporal things and promotion in civil affairs. In boyhood he had felt a deep concern for his eternal interests. The year of his marriage he wrote:

"Come, blest religion,
   with thy angel's face,
Dispel this gloom, and brighten
   all the place;
Drive this destructive passion
   from my breast;
Compose my sorrows, and restore
   my rest;
Show me the path that Christian
   heroes trod;
Wean me from earth, and raise my
   soul to God!"

But before this prayer received fruition, the longings it expressed were well-nigh banished. Friends placed in his hands the works of Paine, Voltaire, and similar writers, and he was soon an avowed deist. And not content with refusing the gospel, he plunged to the fearful depth of making religion a matter of jest, even mimicking the ministers of God, especially his grandfather and his uncle Elihu Miller. But again we are reminded of the efficacy of prayer. These two very men made Miller's case a special subject of prayer; and to his almost heart-broken mother, the grandfather said: "Don't afflict yourself too deeply about William. There is something for him to do yet in the cause of God."

Twelve long years his heart withstood the siege of Heaven's gentle artillery. During this time he served as captain in the War of 1812. Here an incident occurred that showed his attitude toward religion. There were a few men of prayer in the ungodly camp. In the tent of one of these, a sergeant, a meeting was held one night when Captain Miller was in charge. Seeing the tent lighted up, he drew near and heard the voice of prayer. Next day, thinking to try the sergeant's piety, and indulge himself in a joke, he called the man before him, and with seeming seriousness said: "You know, Sergeant Willey, that it is contrary to army regulations to have any gambling in the tents at night; and I was sorry to see your tent lighted up for that purpose last night. We can not have any gambling at such times. You must put a stop to it at once. I hope I shall not have to speak to you again about it!"

The poor man stood as if thunderstruck; and then, hardly daring to look up, replied, in a manner which showed unwillingness to bear the scandal of gambling or to parade his devotions, "We were not gambling, sir."

The captain was touched with his appearance, but affected even greater severity. "What else could you have your tent lighted up for all the evening if you were not gambling?"

In a deeply impressive manner, the accused at last confessed his grief and innocence: "We were praying, sir."

An unseen Presence was so sensibly manifest that the captain was almost moved to tears. He silently dismissed the man with a wave of the hand, and for some time sat in reverent contemplation of the bloodless battle he had planned, but which, with other experiences in the war, served to weaken his infidelity.

On returning home, he moved amid his infidel friends; but the time had come when the prayers of long years of waiting were about to be answered. God was about to call him to another kind of warfare. His feelings he thus described:

"The heavens were as brass over my head, and the earth as iron under my feet. Eternity—what was it? And death—why was it? The more I reasoned, the farther I was from demonstration. The more I thought, the more scattered were my conclusions. I tried to stop thinking; but my thoughts would not be controlled....Suddenly the character of a Saviour was vividly impressed upon my mind. It seemed that there might be a Being so good and compassionate as to Himself atone for our transgressions, and thereby save us from suffering the penalty of sin. I immediately felt how lovely such a Being must be, and imagined that I could cast myself into the arms of, and trust in the mercy of, such a One....I saw that the Bible did bring to view just such a Saviour as I needed; and...I was constrained to admit that the Scriptures must be a revelation from God....The Bible now became my chief study, and I can truly say I searched it with great delight. I found the half was never told me. I wondered why I had not seen its beauty and glory before, and marveled that I could have ever rejected it....I lost all taste for other reading, and applied my heart to get wisdom from God."

But his friends were quick to present objections he had often urged. He determined to be able to meet them. He allowed the Bible to be its own interpreter. As he studied with earnest prayer for divine enlightenment, the books of Daniel and Revelation finally engaged his special attention. To his surprise and delight he found their strange prophetic symbols could be understood; and his attention finally became riveted upon the great end of their panoramic display; namely, the grand doctrine of the second coming of the Son of God.

Eighteen hundred years before, when the gates of the eternal city, were about to open to receive from earth our ascending Lord, two angels in shining raiment stood by the little group on Olive's brow, and made an announcement which thrilled the hearts of the listeners. That announcement has been a joy to earth's lowly ones through the ages since: *"This same Jesus... shall so come in like manner as ye have seen him go into heaven."* This bright arch of hope spans the entrance to the book of Acts, and is the great theme of the book of Revelation, and *"the end of the matter"* in the book of Daniel. Beneath its halo our student stood until the joy that filled the hearts of the first disciples was his. This glad hope is the object and end of many an inspired prophecy; and in these William Miller felt that he had found a clue to the time of the great event. Here are his words:

"I could but regard the chronological portions of the Bible as being as much a portion of the word of God, and as much entitled to our serious consideration, as any other portion of the Scriptures. I therefore felt that in endeavoring to comprehend what God had in His mercy seen fit to reveal to us, I had no right to pass over the prophetic periods." "The seventy weeks to the Messiah (Dan. 9:24-27—7 days to the week, equal 490 days) were fulfilled in 490 years; and the 1,260 prophetic days (Rev. 11:3) of the papal supremacy, in 1,260 years.... From a further study of the Scriptures I concluded...that the 2,300 days (Dan. 8:14) commenced with the seventy weeks, which the best chronologers dated B.C. 457, and that the 1,335 days (Dan. 12:12) should be dated from about A.D. 508. Reckoning all these prophetic periods from the several dates assigned by the best chronologers for the events from which they should evidently be reckoned, they would all terminate together about A.D. 1843."

Believing with others that the earth was *"the sanctuary"* referred to, which was to be *"cleansed,"* he came to the conclusion that about the last date named, the Judge of all the earth would come. "I need not speak of the joy that filled my heart in view of the delightful prospect, nor of the ardent longings of my soul for a participation in the joys of the redeemed. The Bible was now to me a new book. It was indeed a feast."

He united with the Baptist Church, which later licensed him to preach. For years he gave the subject of Christ's second coming much study, and so carefully was every argument weighed, that he was prepared to meet every objection before he went upon the platform. Indeed, he long resisted the call to the ministry. "The question came home to me with mighty power," he says, "regarding my duty to the world, in view of the evidence that had affected my own mind." "When I was about my business, it was continually ringing in my ears, 'Go and tell the world of their danger.' This text was constantly occurring to me: *If thou dost not speak to warn the wicked from his way, that wicked man shall die in his iniquity; but his blood will I require at thine hand.'*

"I did all I could to avoid the conviction that anything was required of me....I told the Lord that I was not used to public speaking; that I had not the necessary qualifications to gain the attention of an audience....But I could get no relief."

He tried to satisfy his conscience by speaking in private of his views, hoping some one would be raised up to proclaim them to the world. He was quite surprised and grieved to find but few, even of professed Christians, who were vitally interested in the subject. "I supposed that it would call forth the opposition of the ungodly; but it never came into my mind that any Christian would oppose it. I supposed that all such would be so rejoiced in view of the glorious prospect, that it would be only necessary to pres-

ent it to them for them to receive it." Imagine his feelings, then, when it came to his ears that a friend of his, a physician, had said, "Esquire Miller is a fine man and a good neighbor, but is a monomaniac on the subject of the advent."

A little later one of Mr. Miller's children was sick, and the doctor was called. After prescribing for the child, the doctor noticed that Mr. Miller was very quiet, and inquired what ailed him.

"Well, I hardly know, doctor; I want you to see what does, and prescribe for me."

The doctor felt of his pulse, and asked what he supposed was his complaint.

"Well," said Mr. Miller, "I don't know but I am a monomaniac....Can you tell when a man is a monomaniac?"

The doctor blushed, and said he thought he could.

"Well," said Mr. Miller, "I insist upon it that you see whether I am in reality a monomaniac; and if I am, you shall prescribe for and cure me. You shall, therefore, sit down with me two hours, while I present the subject of the advent to you; and if I am a monomaniac, by that time you will discover it."

The doctor was quite disconcerted; but Mr. Miller insisted, and said he might charge for his time as in his regular practise.

The doctor finally sat down, took a Bible, and at Mr. Miller's request, read from the 8th of Daniel. As he read, Mr. Miller inquired what "the ram" denoted; also the other symbols. The doctor had read Newton, and applied them to Persia, Greece, and Rome, as did Mr. Miller.

Mr. Miller then asked him how long the vision of those empires was to be. "Twenty-three hundred days."

"What!" said Mr. Miller; "could those great empires cover only 2,300 literal days?"

"Why," said the doctor, "those days are years, according to all commentators; and those kingdoms are to continue 2,300 years."

Mr. Miller then asked him to turn to the 2nd and 7th of Daniel, both of which he explained as Mr. Miller did. He was then asked if he knew when the 2,300 days would end. He did not, as he could not tell when they began. He was asked to read the 9th of Daniel. As he read the 21st verse, mentioning Gabriel,

"seen in the vision," Mr. Miller inquired:

"In what vision?"

"Why," said the doctor, "in the vision of the 8th of Daniel."

"He had now come, then, to make him understand that vision, had he?"

"Yes."

"Well; seventy weeks are determined; what are these seventy weeks a part of?"

"Of the 2,300 days."

"Then do they begin with the 2,300 days?"

"Yes."

"When did they end?"

"In A.D. 33."

"Then how far would the 2,300 extend after A.D. 33?"

The doctor subtracted 490 (the number of days in "seventy weeks") from 2,300, and replied, "1810." "Why!" said he, "that is past!"

"But," said Mr. Miller, "there were 1,810 from 33; in what year would that come?"

The doctor set down 33 and 1,810, and adding, replied, "1843." With flushed face at this unexpected result, he immediately took his hat and left the house. The doctor had not the least idea of the result to which he was coming until he set down the figures 1843.

The next day he called on Mr. Miller in deep agitation, and said: "I have not slept a wink since I was here yesterday. I have looked at the question in every light, and the vision must terminate about 1843; and I am unprepared!"

Pointing him to the One whose coming he loved, Mr. Miller labored for him till he too loved His coming.

But to go and stand before the public as he felt the Lord was calling him to do, seemed to Mr. Miller an impossibility. Finally, one morning in August, 1831, as he arose from his chair to go to his work, it came to him with more force than ever, "Go and tell it to the world!"

"The impression was so sudden," says the man under conviction, "and came with such force, that I settled down in my chair, saying, 'I can't go, Lord.'"

"Why not?" seemed to be the response.

"Then all my excuses came up—my want of ability, etc., but my distress became so great I entered into a solemn covenant with God that if He would open the way, I would go and perform my duty to the world.

" 'What do you mean by opening the way!' seemed to come to me.

" 'Why,' said I, 'if I should have an invitation to speak publicly in any place, I will go and tell them what I find in the Bible about the Lord's coming.'

"Instantly all my burden was gone, and I rejoiced that I should not probably be thus called upon; for I had never had such an invitation."

But what was his surprise and dismay when, before he left the room, a young man living at Dresden, sixteen miles away, came to his door, and said his father had sent him to have Mr. Miller come to present his views in their church the next day. He was so overcome, he left the boy without a reply, and retired to a grove in great distress. "There," said he, "I struggled with the Lord about an hour, endeavoring to release myself from the covenant I had made with Him; but I could get no relief. It was impressed upon my conscience, 'Will you make a covenant with God and break it so soon?' and the exceeding sinfulness of thus doing overwhelmed me."

At last he yielded, and went to the appointment. Tho house was well filled; and as might be expected, as soon as he commenced speaking, his embarrassment was gone. He was requested to remain and lecture during the week; and a revival was begun in which thirteen families, except two persons, were converted.

He returned home only to find a letter to come to another point, from one who did not know he had gone to Dresden. Then invitations poured in upon him, more than he could fill. His labors became extensive, and he defrayed his own expenses. Up to 1836 two half dollars placed in his hand by a woman in Canada was the only contribution he received. Touching this point, he wrote to a friend: "How good, my brother, it is to preach, having God for paymaster! He pays down! He pays in souls!"

Of an eight days' meeting held in Lansingburg, New York, he wrote: "Infidels, deists, Universalists, and sectarians, were all chained to their seats, in perfect silence for hours, yes, days, to hear the stammering

old man talk about the second coming of Christ, and show the manner, object, time, and signs, of His coming. O my brother! it makes me feel like a worm—a poor, feeble creature; for it is God only who could produce such an effect on such audiences."

Of the results following lectures in Portsmouth, New Hampshire, the pastor of the Christian Church published the following: "Never, while we linger on the shores of mortality, do we expect to enjoy more of heaven than we have in some of our late meetings, and on baptizing occasions. At the waterside, thousands would gather to witness this solemn institution in Zion, and many would return from the place weeping."

The following is from a notice appearing in the *Fountain,* New Haven, Connecticut, after lectures there: "We were utterly disappointed—so many extravagant things have been said of the 'fanatics' in the public prints, and such distorted statements published in reference to their articles of faith....In justice to Mr. Miller, we are constrained to say that he is one of the most interesting lecturers we have any recollection of ever having heard."

Those who have followed the footprints of our heroes in previous chapters are not surprised to know that, like them, Miller received his full share of the world's scorn. Some of it came from without the church; some of it from within. In self-defense he finally published an appeal:

"Dear Brethren: We would ask, in the name of our dear Master, Jesus Christ, by all that is holy, by the fellowship of the saints, and the love of the truth, why you cast us off as if we were heretics. What have we believed that we have not been commanded to believe by the word of God?...Is it heterodox to believe that Jesus Christ will come again to this earth to receive His saints to Himself, and to reward all men as their work shall be? If so, then our fathers, and our ministers, our creeds, and our Bibles, have taught us heresy....Do tell us what mean a class of texts like these: John 14:3; Acts 1:11; I Peter 1:7, 13; Revelation 1:7....Are we not all commanded to watch?...If so, will you tell us how a man can watch, and not expect the object for which he watches?...If we are to be cut off for honestly believing in the exactness of prophetic time, then Scott and Wesley, and the Newtons, and Mede, Gill, and others, should all be excommunicated for the like offense."

There were not a few, however, whose honest words should have put to shame all those who heaped contumely upon his devoted head. Witness the following from the Sandy Hill *Herald*, a paper published in Mr. Miller's home county:

"Certainly all who have ever heard him lecture, or have read his works, must acknowledge that he is a sound reasoner....Mr. Miller is now, and has been for many years, a resident of this county, and as a citizen, a man, and a Christian, stands high in the estimation of all who know him; and we have been pained to hear the grayheaded, trembling old man denounced as a 'speculating knave.'

"Speculating, forsooth! Why need he speculate?...Who that has witnessed his earnestness in the pulpit, and listened to the uncultivated eloquence of nature, which falls in such rich profusion from his lips, dare say that he is an impostor? We answer without fear of contradiction from any candid mind, None!...

"Mr. Miller certainly goes to the fountain of knowledge—revelation and history—for proof, and should not be answered with low, vulgar, and blasphemous witticisms."

This paper then quoted from an exchange as follows: "To treat a subject of such overwhelming majesty and fearful consequences—a subject which has been made the theme of prophecy in both Testaments; the truth of which, occur when it will, God has sealed by His own unequivocal averments—we repeat it, to make puns and display vulgar wit upon this subject, is not merely to sport with the feelings of its propagators and advocates, but is to make a jest of the day of Judgment, to scoff at the Deity Himself, and to contemn the terrors of His Judgment-bar."

The editor of the *Gazette and Advertiser,* of Williamsburg, Long Island, referred to an interview with him as follows:

"Our curiosity was recently gratified by an introduction to this gentleman, who has probably been an object of more abuse, ridicule, and blackguardism, than any other man now living....When our interview closed, we were left wondering at the cause of that malignant spirit of slander and falsehood with which a man has been assailed, who has spent his time and substance in a course of unceasing toils to persuade men 'to flee from the wrath to come.'"

The words of one who has learned to look beneath the surface are very applicable here:

"God's born prophets must not be disobedient to the heavenly vision, though others see not the form and hear not the voice....The men that are the martyrs to the hatred and violence of one age, are the saints that a succeeding age canonizes. Would that we might not slay God's prophets, leaving a wiser generation to pay its too tardy tribute at their sepulchers!"

Mr. Miller never went where he was not invited; and the invitations usually came from the ministers of the different denominations. Conversions and revivals almost invariably followed his ministrations.

The manner in which he met an intended slight was shown at Lowell, Massachusetts. A minister there had heard of the great success attending his lectures, and invited him to come to his church. On meeting the train, he saw no such fashionably dressed gentleman as he expected, but a plainly clad old man, shaking with palsy. He feared this might prove to be the man, and if so, regretted having invited him to his fashionable church. He stepped up to him, however, and whispered in his ear, "Is your name Miller?"

The old gentleman nodded assent.

"Well, follow me," he said, walking on, leaving Mr. Miller to get along as best he could. He was much chagrined that he had invited a man of such appearance to speak in his church, concluding that he could know little of the Scriptures, and would discourse upon fancies of his own.

After tea he remarked that he supposed it was about time to attend church; and again leading the way, he left Mr. Miller to bring up the rear. After showing him into the desk, he himself took a seat in the congregation.

The trembling old man read a hymn, which was sung. He then led in prayer, and read another hymn, which was also sung. Opening with reverence the Book of God, which had now for long years been his consolation and support, he took for his text, *"Looking for that blessed hope, and the glorious appearing of the great God and our Saviour Jesus Christ."* Like the man of God that he was, rising on the wings of his theme, far above the chilling atmosphere of pride and prejudice, as one illumined with light from on high, the speaker launched forth upon his subject to picture the glories of *"that hope"* that leads to the better land.

The minister listened while there poured forth from once unwilling lips, now touched, as it were, by seraphim's fingers, such words of burning eloquence as lifted the thoughts far from the plain dress of the speaker. Forgetting the difference in outward adorning, and rising from his place in the audience, the pastor walked into the pulpit, and took his seat. The lectures were continued for more than a week, while over the parapets of prejudice and unbelief, charge after charge was made, and the crimson colors were unfurled above the crumbling walls of infidelity. The minister embraced Mr. Miller's views in full, baptized forty converts, received sixty members; and still others were moved to seek the Lord.

The poet Whittier attended a camp-meeting where Miller delivered a course of lectures, and wrote a vivid description, where the speaker "followed the music with an earnest exhortation on the duty of preparing for the great event. Occasionally he was really eloquent, and his description of the last day had all the terrible distinctness of Anelli's painting of the 'End of the World.'"

When Lafayette visited America, Mr. Miller met him and dined with him, and wrote a pleasing description of that "friend of freemen" and "terror to tyrants."

While Mr. Miller was lecturing in Philadelphia, a friend gave the following of him:

"There is a kindness of soul, simplicity, and power, peculiarly original, combined in his manner; and he is affable and attentive to all, without any affectation of superiority....His countenance is full and round, while there is a peculiar expression in his blue eyes, of shrewdness and **love**....In his social relations, he is gentle and affectionate, and insures the esteem of all with whom he mingles."

Only two years after Mr. Miller began to present his views publicly, there occurred a striking fulfilment of prophecy. When Jesus was with His disciples, they came to Him and asked, *"What shall be the sign of thy coming, and of the end of the world?"* He did not rebuke them, nor say, "Of this you can know nothing;" but in answer He gave them three great signs which were to be hung out in the heavens,—the darkening of the sun and moon, and the falling of the stars. The first two took place May 19, 1780; and the latter, November 13, 1833, in the great display of falling meteors. From two o'clock in the morning until broad daylight, over all North America, the whole heavens seemed to be in fiery commotion. Many interesting descriptions have been recorded. One wrote of it, "It seemed as if the whole starry heavens had congregated at one point near the zenith, and were simultaneously shooting forth, with the velocity of lightning, to every part of the horizon, and yet were not exhausted—thousands swiftly followed by thousands, as if created for the occasion."

Thus occurred the third of the great signs of which Jesus said, *"When ye shall see all these things, know that it* ["He," margin] *is near, even at the doors."* Many looked upon the event at the time as a herald of the coming Judgment,— "an awful type, a sure forerunner, a merciful sign, of that great and dreadful day." It seemed as if, in this great sign, heaven would display its celestial splendors in confirmation of its movings upon the hearts of men. Many beheld the scene with terror; others with calm confidence that God was fulfilling His word, that He was setting His seal to the spiritual work He was leading His servants to perform.

As if evidence would be given mountain high, until the world would stand in awe and without excuse, in the year 1840 the pencil of history was compelled to trace another wonderful fulfilment of prophecy. In 1838, a minister named Josiah Litch, who had united with Miller in the work, published an exposition of verses 10 and 15 of Revelation 9, reckoning a day as standing for a literal year, and predicting the very year and month in which the Turkish government would surrender its independence; namely, August 11, 1840. Referring to the expiration of the combined periods of those two verses, his words were, "In A.D. 1840, sometime in the month of August;" and before the event occurred, he published the very date, August 11, 1840.

What is the testimony of history? Thousands watched to see if such a thing would come to pass. In 1839, the Turkish army was defeated by Mehemet Ali. England, Russia, Austria, and Prussia, seeing that he was about to triumph over the sultan of Turkey, stepped in to prevent it and to settle the difficulty. They drew up an ultimatum, which was to stay Mehemet's course. This was placed in his hands August 11, 1840!

A note was on that very day addressed by the sultan to the powers, inquiring what course he should pursue in case Mehemet should refuse to accept the ultimatum. They replied to the effect that they would attend to that. Thus the independence of the Turkish empire was ended on the very day predicted in the prophecy. And to this day, the government of "the sick man of the East" stands only by the sufferance of those nations, as is well known to every student of their history.

This striking fulfilment of prophecy, and its exact interpretation, coming in just at the right time, gave a mighty impetus to the work in which Miller was engaged. Invitations more than he could possibly accept poured in upon him from the ministers of other denominations, and vast audiences listened as if a spell from heaven had fallen upon them.

All these mighty evidences are just as potent to-day as in the day of their fulfilment. They are matters of history, and a part of God's everlasting truth; and it is a great wonder that they have been so lost from sight. Let His messengers everywhere hurl them against the efforts of the "higher critics" and the lower critics who try to overthrow God's word.

A very interesting and convincing feature of that stirring period, was that in different countries, the proclamation of the near coming of the Master was made without any knowledge of the work of Miller. Indeed, it began in England as early as 1826. It was taught in Germany, France, Switzerland, and in South America. It was heard in Scandinavia; and as it was opposed by the state clergy there, an authentic record of its progress says: "God was pleased to send the message, in a miraculous manner, through little children. As they were under age, the law of the state could not restrain them, and they were permitted to speak unmolested.... Some of them were not more than six or eight years of age; and while their lives testified that they loved the Saviour, and were trying to live in obedience to God's holy requirements, they ordinarily manifested only the intelligence and ability usually seen in children of that age. When standing before the people, however, it was evident they were moved by an influence beyond their own natural gifts. Tone and manner changed, and with solemn power they gave the warning of the Judgment, employing the very words of Scripture, *'Fear God, and give glory to him; for the hour of his Judgment is come.'*...The people heard with trembling. The convicting Spirit of God spoke to their hearts." (*Great Controversy*)

Of that time, when it was expected that the Saviour's coming was at hand, Mr. Miller wrote: "There is no great expression of joy; that is, as it were, suppressed for a future occasion, when all heaven and earth will rejoice together with joy unspeakable and full of glory. There is no shouting; that, too, is reserved for the shout from heaven. The singers are silent; they are waiting to join the angelic hosts, the choir from heaven....The general expression is, *'Behold, the Bridegroom cometh! Go ye out to meet him!'*"

The great prophetic watchtower upon which Miller built his brightest beacon was Daniel 8:14, *"Unto two thousand and three hundred days; then shall the sanctuary be cleansed."* When the movement had been making wonderful progress, it was discovered that the commandment of Daniel 9:25, which fixes the beginning of this period, was not executed until part of the year 457 B.C. had expired, and therefore 2,300 full years would extend into the year 1844. But the years 1843 and 1844 came and went; and the One whom Miller loved and served came not to earth. Like Mary, who stood at the rent sepulcher, so Miller and his fellow laborers were deeply disappointed; but they loved their Lord no less. Mary was mistaken, but she was no fanatic.

"Were I to live my life over again," wrote Mr. Miller, "with the same evidence that I then had, to be honest with God and man, I should have to do as I have done....I still believe that the day of the Lord is near, even at the door; and I exhort you, my brethren, to be watchful, and not let that day come upon you unawares."

And now, in view of the superabundance of evidence that the movement was of God, what about the disappointment! Ah, though this was bitter and hard to bear, it was not so keen and cutting as was that of the first disciples when the throne of their King was a cross, His scepter a reed, His crown a wreath of thorns! But both disappointments are explained by the same infallible Word. Let us *be not faithless, but believing."*

The prophecy whose time period ended in 1844 had said, *"Then shall the sanctuary be cleansed."* A careful study of the subject of the sanctuary reveals the fact that *"the sanctuary," "the true tabernacle,"* is in heaven, where Christ is now our High Priest; and that its cleansing

is a work of judgment, blotting out of sins, and appointing of rewards.

With this agrees the announcement in that solemn hour, placed even upon the lips of children, *"Fear God, and give glory to him; for the hour of his Judgment is come"* (Revelation 14:7). Thus since 1844, it has been, and now is, court week in heaven. Before that great and decisive tribunal the destiny of each individual will be determined. When the rewards for His children are all appointed, then Christ will come, to give to every man as his work shall be (Revelation 22:12), and to take His people to the mansions He has gone to prepare.

Revelation 10 is clearly prophetic of the opening of *"the little book"* of Daniel, which had been *"closed up and sealed till the time of the end"* (Daniel 12:9). The foundation pillar of Miller's work is found in that book. The feeding upon that book, the sweet satisfaction that came from it, and the bitter disappointment as well, are all pointed out in this 10th of Revelation, verses 8-10. And that all this was to be followed by a further preaching of prophecy, is evident from verse 11, *"Thou must prophesy again before many people, and nations, and tongues, and kings."*

The great God intends that the world shall hear His word proclaiming the event of the ages—the coming of His Son, the *"King of kings, and Lord of lords."* And this sublime announcement stands as a mighty prelude to the great closing drama, as an index-finger pointing to the Saviour's sign-board,—*"This gospel of the kingdom shall be preached in all the world for a witness unto all nations; and then shall the end come."*

The last and longest prophetic period has ended. The Saviour's sign is significant and sufficient. With this understanding of the prophetic word, how appropriate and indispensable was the work of Miller! How many more ought to labor, and ever since have been laboring, as he did! And what new motives for missions awake in our hearts as we enter the mines he explored and disclosed!

Until 1849 this devoted man lived to labor and long for his Master's coming. Near the close of life he wrote: "On recalling to mind the several places of my labors, I can reckon up about six thousand instances of conversion from nature's darkness to God's marvelous light.... Of this number I can recall to mind about seven hundred who were, previously to attending my lectures,

infidels, and their number may have been twice as great."

From his dying pillow he sent forth the message, "The coming of the Lord draweth nigh; but we must be patient and wait for Him!" How different the retrospect of such a life from that of one who knows not God! And if God would take such a one—an infidel, who knew not and **loved** not Him—and make of him such a mouthpiece for Himself, will He not make of us what He would have us be, that our hearts may become as sacred harps to sound His praise to earth's remotest bounds?

The following tribute to Mr. Miller's memory is by one who knew him: "However roughly and wickedly men may have handled the name of William Miller here, when the final triumphant deliverance of all who are written in the book of life comes, his will be found among the worthies, safe from the wrath of men and the rage of demons, securing to him the reward of immortality according to his works."

We pause, in taking leave of William Miller, to ask the meaning of all these converging lines of light. Was it not that another "birth-hour" in the life of humanity has struck? Do not its tidings even now tremble upon the tongue of time, waiting to tell that Messiah is near? Was it not another hour very like that when Judea should have run the earth with the welcome to her Lord, but, instead, plunged past Him to her ruin, not knowing the time of her visitation? Was it not an invitation and a warning to prepare for the heavenly Canaan? and have we not paused these years in the wilderness, and in heart returned to Egypt and refused the goodly land?

Whatever answers we may determine upon, it must needs be that some of God's sentinels are upon His watchtowers, and behold in the east the tokens of His coming; and soon there will be trumpeted from lip to lip and from heart to heart the cry, *"Behold, the Bridegroom cometh; go ye out to meet him!"* The handwriting is upon the wall; its interpreters are in waiting. The Conqueror comes to rend the kingdoms of the world from the prince of darkness, that the scepter of righteousness may be swayed by His hand whose right it is!

Away back in the ages, God wrote above the palace of the proud Pharaohs, in the persons of His representatives, *"Thou shalt have no other gods before me."* But little did those monarchs learn or discern the heavenly vision; and as soon as a human tongue was ready to

deliver God's message, He led His people forth. If it should be that you have been cast beside some shoreless sea, only let its waters become a wall and a way to shut out all else but Israel's invisible Leader; and as we enter the wilderness beyond, let every voice be hushed but His which spoke from Sinai's height, before whom Moses bowed and did *"exceedingly fear and quake."*

And if, while in the way, we are brought face to face with Scripture teaching unknown or ignored in the past, let us, like Miller, be too honest to compromise, too brave to turn back. If our fine library of commentaries sinks to the bottom of the sea, as did Duff's, the Bible alone remaining, or goes up in the smoke of untenable theories, as Butler's books were burned in his mission home, let us make and hold to the resolve that we will follow the flaming wake of the Spirit's sword, the word of God. And those who truly follow it shall not walk in darkness, but shall have the light of life.

Then, looking upon the world no longer as a prize to be grasped by the spirit of greed, but in the light that flows down the mystic ladder of a Saviour's love, let our lives be poured out upon the altar of missions or in the furrows of the nearest need.

There are yet mighty men of valor, flailing out a few kernels of wheat behind the wine-press, only waiting the signal of God's angels to step forth girded with *"the sword of the Lord and of Gideon,"* to follow on, even though sometimes faint, yet pursuing, until earth's ends are lighted with the lamps in the broken pitchers.

Let the thousands of fearful and faint-hearted remain at home. Let those who can not bear the tests of self-denial and sacrifice in service be counted out. God has His more than three hundred who will take no glory to themselves; yea, more than seven thousand who have not bowed the knee to Baal nor kissed him, through whom He will lead His legions on, and on, and on, to certain victory!*

How different
are God's ways
from man's!

*The Advance Guard
of Missions 324-347

History of the Schools of the Prophets

"But the wisdom that is from above
is first pure, then peaceable, gentle, and easy to be entreated,
full of mercy and good fruits, without partiality and without hypocrisy."
James 3:17

"The fear of the LORD is the beginning of wisdom:
and the knowledge of the Holy is understanding."
Proverbs 9:10

Schools of the Prophets = SOP
SOP = Spirit of Prophecy

Research
The Schools of the Prophets

"The Lord Himself directed the education of Israel. His care was not restricted to their religious interests; whatever affected their mental or physical well-being was also the subject of divine providence, and came within the sphere of divine law.

"God had commanded the Hebrews to teach their children His requirements and to make them acquainted with all His dealings with their fathers. This was one of the special duties of every parent—one that was not to be delegated to another. In the place of stranger lips the loving hearts of the father and mother were to give instruction to their children. <u>Thoughts of God were to be associated with all the events of daily life. The mighty works of God in the deliverance of His people and the promises of the Redeemer to come were to be often recounted in the homes of Israel; and the use of figures and symbols caused the lessons given to</u> <u>be more firmly fixed in the memory. The great truths of God's providence and of the future life were impressed on the young mind.</u> It was trained to see God alike in the scenes of nature and the words of revelation. The stars of heaven, the trees and flowers of the field, the lofty mountains, the rippling brooks—all spoke of the Creator. The solemn service of sacrifice and worship at the sanctuary and the utterances of the prophets were a revelation of God.

"God had commanded the Hebrews to teach their children His requirements and <u>to make them acquainted with all His dealings with their fathers.</u>"

"Such was the training of Moses in the lowly cabin home in Goshen; of Samuel, by the faithful Hannah; of David, in the hill dwelling at Bethlehem; of Daniel, before the scenes of the captivity separated him from the home of his fathers. Such, too, was the early life of Christ at Nazareth; such the training by which the child Timothy learned from the lips of his grandmother Lois, and his mother Eunice (II Timothy 1:5; 3:15), the truths of Holy Writ.

"Further provision was made for the instruction of the young, by the establishment of the schools of the prophets. If a youth desired to search deeper into the truths of the word of God and to seek **wisdom** from above, that he might become a teacher in Israel, these schools were open to him. The schools of the prophets were founded by Samuel to serve as a barrier against the widespread corruption, to provide for the moral and spiritual welfare of the youth, and to promote the future prosperity of the nation by furnishing it with men qualified to act in the fear of God as leaders and counselors. In the accomplishment of this object Samuel gathered companies of young men who were pious, intelligent, and studious. These were called the sons of the prophets. As they communed with God and studied His word and His works, **wisdom** from above was added to their natural endowments. The instructors were men not only well versed in divine truth, but those who had themselves enjoyed communion with God and had received the special endowment of His Spirit. They enjoyed the respect and confidence of the people, both for learning and piety.

Child Jesus had His school at home.

"The schools of the prophets were founded by Samuel to serve as a barrier against the widespread corruption, to provide for the moral and spiritual welfare of the youth, and to promote the future prosperity of the nation by furnishing it with men qualified to act in the fear of God as leaders and counselors."

Even so late as the time of the apostles, Paul and Aquila were no less honored because they earned a livelihood by their trade of tentmaking.

"In Samuel's day there were two of these schools—one at Ramah, the home of the prophet, and the other at Kirjath-jearim, where the ark then was. Others were established in later times.

"<u>The pupils of these schools sustained themselves by their own labor in tilling the soil or in some mechanical employment</u>. In Israel this was not thought strange or degrading; indeed, it was regarded a crime to allow children to grow up in ignorance of useful labor. <u>By the command of God every child was taught some trade, even though he was to be educated for holy office</u>. Many of the religious teachers supported themselves by manual labor.

"<u>The chief subjects of study in these schools were the law of God, with the instructions given to Moses, sacred history, sacred music, and poetry</u>. The manner of instruction was far different from that in the theological schools of the present day, from which many students graduate with less real knowledge of God and religious truth than when they entered. <u>In those schools of the olden time it was the grand object of all study to learn the will of God and man's duty toward Him. In the records of sacred history were traced the **footsteps of Jehovah**. The great truths set forth by the types were brought to view, and faith grasped the central object of all that system—the Lamb of God that was to take away the sin of the world</u>.

"A spirit of devotion was cherished. <u>Not only were students taught the duty of prayer, but they were taught how to pray, how to approach their Creator, how to exercise faith in Him, and how to understand and obey the teachings of His Spirit</u>. Sanctified intellects brought forth from the treasure house of God things new and old, and <u>the Spirit of God was manifested in prophecy and sacred song</u>.

"Music was made to serve a holy purpose, to lift the thoughts to that which is <u>pure, noble, and elevating, and to awaken in the soul devotion and gratitude to God</u>. What a contrast between the ancient custom and the uses to which music is now too often devoted! How many employ this gift to exalt self, instead of using it to Glorify God! A **love** for music leads the unwary to unite with world lovers in pleasure gatherings where God has forbidden His children to go. Thus that which is a great blessing when rightly used, becomes one of the most successful agencies by which Satan allures the mind from duty and from the contemplation of eternal things.

"<u>Music forms a part of God's worship in the courts above, and we should endeavor, in our songs of praise, to approach as nearly as possible to the harmony of the heavenly choirs. The proper training of the voice is an important feature in education and should not be neglected. Singing, as a part of religious service, is as much an act of worship as is prayer</u>. The heart must feel the spirit of the song to give it right expression.

"**The proper training of the voice is an important feature in education and should not be neglected.**"

"How wide the difference between those schools taught by the prophets of God and our modern institutions of learning! How few schools are to be found that are not governed by the maxims and customs of the world! There is a deplorable lack of proper restraint and judicious discipline. The existing ignorance of God's word among a people professedly Christian is alarming. Superficial talk, mere sentimentalism, passes for instruction in morals and religion. The justice and mercy of God, the beauty of holiness and the sure reward of right doing, the heinous character of sin and the certainty of its terrible results, are not impressed upon the minds of the young. Evil associates are instructing the youth in the ways of crime, dissipation, and licentiousness.

"Are there not some lessons which the educators of our day might learn with profit from the ancient schools of the Hebrews? He who created man has provided for his development in body and mind and soul. Hence, real success in education depends upon the fidelity with which men carry out the Creator's plan.

"The true object of education is to restore the image of God in the soul. In the beginning God created man in His own likeness. He endowed him with noble qualities. His mind was well balanced, and all the powers of his being were harmonious. But the Fall and its effects have perverted these gifts. Sin has marred and well-nigh obliterated the image of God in man. It was to restore this that the plan of salvation was devised, and a life of probation was granted to man. To bring him back to the perfection in which he was first created is the great object of life—the object that underlies every other. It is the work of parents and teachers, in the education of the youth, to co-operate with the divine purpose; and in so doing they are *'laborers together with God'* (II Corinthians 3:9).

"To bring him back to the perfection in which he was first created is the great object of life—the object that underlies every other."

"All the varied capabilities that men possess—of mind and soul and body—are given them by God, to be so employed as to reach the highest possible degree of excellence. But this cannot be a selfish and exclusive culture; for the character of God, whose likeness we are to receive, is benevolence and **love**. Every faculty, every attribute, with which the Creator has endowed us is to be employed for His glory and for the uplifting of our fellow men. And in this employment is found its purest, noblest, and happiest exercise.

"Were this principle given the attention which its importance demands, there would be a radical change in some of the current methods of education. Instead of appealing to pride and selfish ambition, kindling a spirit of emulation, teachers would endeavor to awaken the **love** for goodness and truth and beauty—to arouse the desire for excellence. The student would seek the development of God's gifts in himself, not to excel others, but to fulfill the purpose of the Creator and to receive His likeness. Instead of being directed to mere earthly standards, or being actuated by the desire for self-exaltation, which in itself dwarfs and belittles, the mind would be directed to the Creator, to know Him and to become like Him.

**A Message
for all Teachers
and Students**

"Instead of appealing
to pride and
selfish ambition,
kindling a spirit
of emulation,
teachers would
endeavor
to awaken the <u>love</u>
for goodness and truth
and beauty—
to arouse the desire
for excellence."

" *The fear of the Lord is the beginning of* **wisdom**: *and the knowledge of the Holy is understanding'* (Proverbs 9:10). The great work of life is character building, and a knowledge of God is the foundation of all true education. To impart this knowledge and to mold the character in harmony with it should be the object of the teacher's work. The law of God is a reflection of His character. Hence the psalmist says, *'All thy commandments are righteousness;'* and *'through thy precepts I get understanding'* (Psalm 119:172, 104). God has revealed Himself to us in His word and in the works of creation. Through the volume of inspiration and the book of nature we are to obtain a knowledge of God.

"It is a law of the mind that it gradually adapts itself to the subjects upon which it is trained to dwell. If occupied with commonplace matters only, it will become dwarfed and enfeebled. If never required to grapple with difficult problems, it will after a time almost lose the power of growth. As an educating power the Bible is without a rival. In the word of God the mind finds subject for the deepest thought, the loftiest aspiration. The Bible is the most instructive history that men possess. It came fresh from the fountain of eternal truth, and a divine hand has preserved its purity through all the ages. It lights up the far-distant past, where human research seeks vainly to penetrate.

> **"The great work of life is character building, and a knowledge of God is the foundation of all true education."**

In God's word we behold the power that laid the foundation of the earth and that stretched out the heavens. Here only can we find a history of our race unsullied by human prejudice or human pride. Here are recorded the struggles, the defeats, and the victories of the greatest men this world has ever known. Here the great problems of duty and destiny are unfolded. The curtain that separates the visible from the invisible world is lifted, and we behold the conflict of the opposing forces of good and evil, from the first entrance of sin to the final triumph of righteousness and truth; and all is but a revelation of the character of God. In the reverent contemplation of the truths presented in His word the mind of the student is brought into communion with the infinite mind. Such a study will not only refine and ennoble the character, but it cannot fail to expand and invigorate the mental powers.

"The teaching of the Bible has a vital bearing upon man's prosperity in all the relations of this life. It unfolds the principles that are the cornerstone of a nation's prosperity—principles with which is bound up the well-being of society, and which are the safeguard of the family—principles without which no man can attain usefulness, happiness, and honor in this life, or can hope to secure the future, immortal life. There is no position in life, no phase of human experience, for which the teaching of the Bible is not an essential preparation. Studied and obeyed, the word of God would give to the world men of stronger and more active intellect than will the closest application to all the subjects that human philosophy embraces. It would give men of strength and solidity of character, of keen perception and sound judgment—men who would be an honor to God and a blessing to the world.

"There is no position in life, no phase of human experience, for which the teaching of the Bible is not an essential preparation."

"In the study of the sciences also we are to obtain a knowledge of the Creator. All true science is but an interpretation of the handwriting of God in the material world. Science brings from her research only fresh evidences of the **wisdom and power** of God. Rightly understood, both the book of nature and the written word make us acquainted with God by teaching us something of the **wise** and beneficent laws through which He works.

"The student should be led to see God in all the works of creation. Teachers should copy the example of the Great Teacher, who from the familiar scenes of nature drew illustrations that simplified His teachings and impressed them more deeply upon the minds of His hearers. The birds caroling in the leafy branches, the flowers of the valley, the lofty trees, the fruitful lands, the springing grain, the barren soil, the setting sun gilding the heavens with its golden beams—all served as means of instruction. He connected the visible works of the Creator with the words of life which He spoke, that whenever these objects should be presented to the eyes of His hearers, their thoughts might revert to the lessons of truth He had linked with them.

"**All true science is but an interpretation of the handwriting of God in the material world.**"

"**Teachers should copy the example of the Great Teacher, who from the familiar scenes of nature drew illustrations that simplified His teachings and impressed them more deeply upon the minds of His hearers.**"

"The impress of Deity, manifest in the pages of revelation, is seen upon the lofty mountains, the fruitful valleys, the broad, deep ocean. The things of nature speak to man of his Creator's **love**. He has linked us to Himself by unnumbered tokens in heaven and in earth. This world is not all sorrow and misery. *'God is love,'* is written upon every opening bud, upon the petals of every flower, and upon every spire of grass. Though the curse of sin has caused the earth to bring forth thorns and thistles, there are flowers upon the thistles and the thorns are hidden by roses. All things in nature testify to the tender, fatherly care of our God and to His desire to make His children happy. His prohibitions and injunctions are not intended merely to display His authority, but in all that He does He has the well-being of His children in view. He does not require them to give up anything that it would be for their best interest to retain.

"The opinion which prevails in some classes of society, that religion is not conducive to health or to happiness in this life, is one of the most mischievous of errors. The Scripture says: *'The fear of the Lord tendeth to life: and he that hath it shall abide satisfied'* (Proverbs 19:23). *'What man is he that desireth life, and **loveth** many days, that he may see good? Keep thy tongue from evil, and thy lips from speaking guile. Depart from evil, and do good; seek peace, and pursue it'* (Psalm 34:12-14). The words of **wisdom** *'are life unto those that find them, and health to all their flesh'* (Proverbs 4:22).

"He has linked us to Himself by unnumbered tokens in heaven and in earth."

"True religion brings man into harmony with the laws of God, physical, mental, and moral. It teaches self-control, serenity, temperance. Religion ennobles the mind, refines the taste, and sanctifies the judgment. It makes the soul a partaker of the purity of heaven. Faith in God's **love** and overruling providence lightens the burdens of anxiety and care. It fills the heart with joy and contentment in the highest or the lowliest lot. Religion tends directly to promote health, to lengthen life, and to heighten our enjoyment of all its blessings. It opens to the soul a never-failing fountain of happiness. Would that all who have not chosen Christ might realize that He has something vastly better to offer them that they are seeking for themselves. Man is doing the greatest injury and injustice to his own soul when he thinks and acts contrary to the will of God. No real joy can be found in the path forbidden by Him who knows what is best, and who plans for the good of His creatures. The path of transgression leads to misery and destruction; but **wisdom's** *'ways are ways of pleasantness, and all her paths are peace'* (Proverbs 3:17).

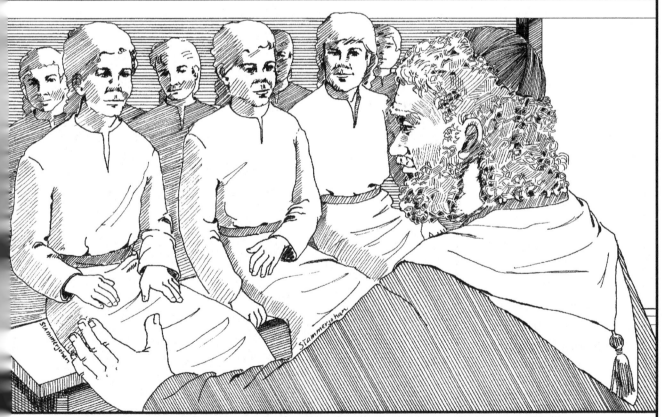

"Would that all who have not chosen Christ might realize that He has something vastly better to offer them that they are seeking for themselves."

"The physical as well as the religious training practiced in the schools of the Hebrews may be profitably studied. The worth of such training is not appreciated. There is an intimate relation between the mind and the body, and in order to reach a high standard of moral and intellectual attainment the laws that control our physical being must be heeded. To secure a strong, well-balanced character, both the mental and the physical powers must be exercised and developed. What study can be more important for the young than that which treats of this wonderful organism that God has committed to us, and of the laws by which it may be preserved in health?

"And now, as in the days of Israel, every youth should be instructed in the duties of practical life. Each should acquire a knowledge of some branch of manual labor by which, if need be, he may obtain a livelihood. This is essential, not only as a safeguard against the vicissitudes of life, but from its bearing upon physical, mental, and moral development. Even if it were certain that one would never need to resort to manual labor for his support, still he should be taught to work. Without physical exercise, no one can have a sound constitution and vigorous health; and the discipline of well-regulated labor is no less essential to the securing of a strong and active mind and a noble character.

> "Even if it were certain that one would never need to resort to manual labor for his support, still he should be taught to work."

"Every student should devote a portion of each day to active labor. Thus habits of industry would be formed and a spirit of self-reliance encouraged, while the youth would be shielded from many evil and degrading practices that are so often the result of idleness. And this is all in keeping with the primary object of education, for in encouraging activity, diligence, and purity we are coming into harmony with the Creator.

"Let the youth be led to understand the object of their creation, to honor God and bless their fellow men; let them see the tender **love** which the Father in heaven has manifested toward them, and the high destiny for which the discipline of this life is to prepare them, the dignity and honor to which they are called, even to become the sons of God, and thousands would turn with contempt and loathing from the low and selfish aims and the frivolous pleasures that have hitherto engrossed them. They would learn to hate sin and to shun it, not merely from hope of reward or fear of punishment, but from a sense of its inherent baseness, because it would be a degrading of their God-given powers, a stain upon their Godlike manhood.

"Every student should devote a portion of each day to active labor. Thus habits of industry would be formed and a spirit of self-reliance encouraged, while the youth would be shielded from many evil and degrading practices that are so often the result of idleness."

"God does not bid the youth to be less aspiring. The elements of character that make a man successful and honored among men—the irrepressible desire for some greater good, the indomitable will, the strenuous exertion, the untiring perseverance—are not to be crushed out. By the grace of God they are to be directed to objects as much higher than mere selfish and temporal interests as the heavens are higher than the earth. And the education begun in this life will be continued in the life to come. Day by day the wonderful works of God, the evidences of His **wisdom** and power in creating and sustaining the universe, the infinite mystery of **love** and **wisdom** in the plan of redemption, will open to the mind in new beauty. *'Eye hath not seen, nor ear heard, neither have entered into the heart of man, the things which God hath prepared for them that **love** him'* (II Corinthians 2:9). Even in this life we may catch glimpses of His presence and may taste the joy of communion with Heaven, but the fullness of its joy and blessing will be reached in the hereafter. Eternity alone can reveal the glorious destiny to which man, restored to God's image, may attain."*

*Patriarchs and Prophets 592-602

"The education begun in this life will be continued in the life to come."

"Even in this life we may catch glimpses of His presence and may taste the joy of communion with Heaven, but the fullness of its joy and blessing will be reached in the hereafter."

"Eternity alone can reveal the glorious destiny to which man, restored to God's image, may attain."

Review
"The Schools of the Prophets"
Place II - III

Home Education

1. Who directed Israel's education?

2. Fill in the blanks with the correct words: "...Whatever _____ their _____ or _____ well-being was also the subject of divine _____, and came within the sphere of divine _____."

3. How and what were the parents to teach the children? What were the children to see about God?

4. Who in the Bible were trained in this way?

Further Education

5. What further instruction was prepared for the young? What kind of children sought these schools? Who founded this school? Why? What were these young people called?

6. How many schools were there in Samuel's time?

7. How did these pupils sustain themselves in school? What other Bible characters sustained themselves by manual labor while they also worked in spiritual lines?

Subjects

8. What chief subjects were taught in these schools? How do they compare with like schools of today?

9. Describe what was cherished in these schools.

10. Tell how music was important in the school of the prophets and how Satan uses it today and why.

Differences

11. What is the difference between the schools of the prophets and modern institutions?

12. Finish this statement: "The true object of education _____ _____ soul." Explain.

True Education

13. Memorize Proverbs 9:10.

14. Fill in the missing words to this statement: "The _____ work of life is _____ _____, and a _____ of God is the _____ of all _____ education."

15. What should be the object of the teacher's work?

The Bible

16. Finish this statement: "It is a law _____
_____
_____
_____
_____
_____
_____
and enfeebled." Explain further.

17. Why is the Bible so vital to education and society?

Sciences

18. What does the study of true science do for man?

19. What is a most mischievous error? What does God say about it?

20. Meditate and discuss this thought with your teacher: "The opinion which prevails in some classes of society, that religion is not conducive to health or to happiness in this life, is one of the most mischievous of errors. The Scripture says: *'The fear of the Lord tendeth to life: and he that hath it shall abide satisfied'* (Proverbs 19:23). *'What man is he that desireth life, and* **loveth** *many days, that he may see good? Keep thy tongue from evil, and thy lips from speaking guile. Depart from evil, and do good; seek peace, and pursue it'* (Psalm 34:12-14). The words of wisdom *'are life unto those that find them, and health to all their flesh.'*"

Physical, Mental, and Spiritual

21. Tell how true religion brings man into harmony with the laws of God.

22. Memorize Proverbs 3:17.

23. Why should we study the physical and religious training in the schools of the prophets?

24. Memorize I Corinthians 2:9.

25. **Thought Question:** What did this section teach you about **wisdom**?

Reinforce

1. Visit a godly homeschool, then a private school classroom, and finally a public school classroom. Compare with the School of the Prophets.

2. Sing the hymn, "I Will Early Seek the Saviour.

3. Make a list of the character qualities in the article about "The Schools of the Prophets."

4. What were the subjects taught in the Schools of the Prophets?

5. Recite Proverbs 9:10, Proverbs 3:17, and I Corinthians 2:9.

6. Read the story, "His Mother's Book."

Remind

1. When doing the food preserving remember you are doing your school work (likewise with gardening, cleaning, building, and _____.)

2. What do you do daily? Remember what was done each day in the Schools of the Prophets.

1 "There is a study of history that is not to be condemned. Sacred history was one of the studies in the schools of the prophets. In the record of His dealings with the nations were traced the <u>footsteps</u> of Jehovah. So today we are to consider the dealings of God

2 with the nations of the earth. We are to see in history the fulfillment of prophecy, to study the workings of Providence in the great reformatory movements, and to understand the progress of events in the marshaling of the nations for the final conflict of the great controversy."*

Counsels to Teachers 379-380

Sacred History Books

'And the LORD said unto Moses,
Write this for a memorial in a book...."
Exodus 17:14

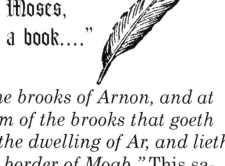

We have no secular history reaching back to the times of the schools of the prophets, established by either Samuel or Elijah, and our only source of knowledge is the history in the Bible. Does the Bible give us any light on the existence of sacred historical books in the days of Samuel, David, Solomon, and Elijah? It does. Following is the information contained in the Bible regarding these sacred history books, with the names of the authors, and the subject matter dealt with in each volume.

Volume 1 – *Book of the Wars
of the Lord*

This book contained a record of the wars fought by Israel during their sojourn in the wilderness. The first mention of this book is found in Exodus 17:14. Moses was asked to preserve a knowledge of the victory gained by Israel over the Amalekites, by writing it *"for a memorial in a book."* The name of this book is given in Numbers 21:14. Here it is declared that *The Book of the Wars of the Lord* contains a record of *"what he* [God] *did in the Red Sea,*

and in the brooks of Arnon, and at the stream of the brooks that goeth down to the dwelling of Ar, and lieth upon the border of Moab." This sacred history volume begins with the victory of the Israelites over the Egyptians at the Red Sea, and probably contains a record of all the battles fought until Israel passed over Jordan into the Promised Land—a record of forty years of war.

Volume 2 – *The Book of Jasher*

After Israel had entered the land of Canaan, they went to war against the Amorites. As the day was not long enough to destroy their enemies completely, Joshua, desiring more time, prayed to the Lord, and *"said in the sight of Israel, Sun, stand thou still upon Gibeon; and thou, Moon, in the valley of Ajalon. And the sun stood still, and the moon stayed, until the people had avenged themselves upon their enemies. Is not this written in the book of Jasher?"* (Joshua 10:12-13).

Just what this book contained is not fully known, but, like *The Book of the Wars of the Lord*, it contains a record of some of the battles of Israel with surrounding nations. *The Book of Jasher* is referred to as containing information concerning the use of the bow in battle; and in David's lamentations over Saul and Jonathan. Mention is made of the children of Judah being taught the use of the bow according to the record contained in *The Book of Jasher* (II Samuel 1:18).

The next three books of the sacred history library treated of the life and times of David.

Volume 3 – *Life and Reign of David*

This book was written by Samuel the seer.

Volume 4 – *Life and Reign of David*

This book was written by Nathan the prophet.

Volume 5 – *Life and Reign of David*

This book was written by Gad the seer.

These three writers were closely associated with David from early boyhood to the end of his reign, and their counsel and advice were eager-ly sought by him in administering the affairs of the kingdom. These were comprehensive volumes; for they covered David's early life, as well as the forty years of his reign and might. They treated also not only of the *"times that went over... Israel"* during the forty years of conquest and subjection of the enemies of Israel, but also of the *"times that went over...all the kingdoms of the countries"* (I Chronicles 29:26-30).

The next three books contain the record of *"the acts of Solomon, and all that he did, and his wisdom,"* covering a period of at least forty years (I Kings 11:41-43). This history of the acts of Solomon is said to have been written by three men, as was also the life and times of David. Each wrote a separate book, so we have three volumes to add to the sacred history library (II Chronicles 9:29).

Volume 6 – *Life and Reign of Solomon*

This volume was written by Nathan the prophet.

Volume 7 – *Life and Reign of Solomon*

This book was written by the prophet Ahijah, the Shilonite.

Volume 8 – *Life and Reign*
of Solomon

The last volume about Solomon was written by Iddo the seer.

Nathan the prophet assisted in writing the history of both David and Solomon. These prophet-historians undoubtedly wrote by inspiration. The six volumes covering the life-work of Israel's two greatest kings, a period of eighty years, must have been filled with very interesting and important matter of the consideration of the sacred history students in the schools of the prophets. The Scriptures do not speak of any history written by a prophet covering the life and reign of Saul. Undoubtedly a daily record of historical events was kept in the royal courts, as is so often referred to by the expressions, *"The book of the chronicles of the kings of Israel," "the book of the kings of Israel and Judah."* But in addition to the records kept in the royal courts by especially appointed secretaries, the Lord in wisdom moved upon certain of the prophets to write the life history and reign of a few of the good kings, and also of a few of the bad kings, that their lives might be studied and pondered by the youth in Israel.

Volume 9 – *The Life and Reign*
of Rehoboam

The life and reign of Rehoboam, son of Solomon, was written in *"the book of the chronicles of the kings of Judah"* (I Kings 14:29); but the Lord had his life and reign also written by two of His prophets, thus adding two more volumes to the sacred history library (II Chronicles 12:15). This volume was written by Shemiah the prophet.

Volume 10 – *Life and Reign*
of Rehoboam

Volume 10 was written by Iddo the seer. The latter volume contained genealogical records which the Lord desired to have preserved for future use.

On the death of Rehoboam, Abijah his son took the throne; after his death, another volume was added to the sacred history library.

Volume 11 – *Life and Reign*
of Abijah

This book was written by Iddo the seer, and contained a record of *"the acts of Abijah, and his ways, and his sayings"* (II Chronicles 13:22). This same prophet wrote Volume 8 on the life of Solomon, and Volume 10 on the life of Rehoboam.

Volume 12 – *Life and Reign of Jehoshaphat*

This volume was written by Jehu, the son of Hanani, and covers the life and reign of Johoshaphat (II Chronicles 20:34). Jehu was a prophet of the Lord, and reproved Jehoshaphat for joining Ahab in war against the Syrians (II Chronicles 19:2). Several kings succeeded Jehoshaphat, of whose reigns no special books were written. All the books written by prophets pertained to the kings of Judah; only the records in the royal courts were written concerning the kings of Israel.

Volume 13 – *Life and Reign of Uzziah*

This book covered Uzziah's reign, a period of fifty years (II Chronicles 26:22). It was written by the prophet Isaiah, the author of the Old Testament book bearing his name. Many important lessons were undoubtedly drawn from the life Uzziah, who was blessed and prospered, but whose heart in his prosperity *"was lifted up to his destruction."*

Volume 14 – *Life and Reign of Hezekiah*

Volume fourteen was also written by the prophet Isaiah, and covered the twenty-nine years of the reign of Hezekiah. This volume contained a complete record of his kind and benevolent administration, and the prosperity that attended his reign (II Chronicles 32:32-33). When Hezekiah died, he was greatly honored, and given the chiefest of the sepulchers as a burying place. A full and complete history of his reign was also recorded in *The Book of the Kings of Judah and Israel.*

In addition to the sacred history library of fourteen volumes, *The Book of the Chronicles of the Kings of Judah* and *The book of the Chronicles of the Kings of Israel* contained valuable material. In extent these writings really embrace many volumes, because they comprehend all the records made in the royal courts regarding the reigns of all the kings of both Judah and Israel. Undoubtedly these records were available to the prophets who taught in the schools of the prophets.

In these royal court volumes were recorded many of the religious as well as secular acts of the kings. With reference to the historical record of King Manasseh, son of Hezekiah, we read:

"Now the rest of the acts of Manasseh, and his prayer unto his God, and the words of the seers that spake to him in the name of the

Lord God of Israel, behold they are written in the book of the kings of Israel. His prayer also, and how God was entreated of him, and all his sins, and his trespass, and the places wherein he built high places, and set up groves and graven images, before he was humbled; behold, they are written among the sayings of the seers" (II Chronicles 33:18-19).

Surely from the Bible we glean abundant evidence of a thorough, complete course of instruction in sacred history as taught in the schools of the prophets. The fourteen volumes written by the prophets were sufficient for the pupils to gain broad, comprehensive views of *"the times that went...over Israel, and over all the kingdoms of the countries"* (I Chronicles 29:30).

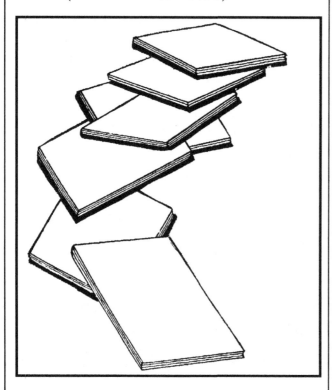

Overview of the Sacred History Library

Volume 1 – *Book of the Wars of the Lord* by Moses (Exodus 17:14)

Volume 2 – *The Book of Jasher* by Joshua (Joshua 10:12-13)

Volume 3 – *Life and Reign of David* by Samuel the seer (I Chronicles 29:29)

Volume 4 – *Life and Reign of David* by Nathan the prophet

Volume 5 – *Life and Reign of David* by Gad the seer

Volume 6 – *Life and Reign of Solomon* by Nathan the prophet (I Kings 11:41-43; II Chronicles 9:29)

Volume 7 – *Life and Reign of Solomon* by Ahijah the prophet

Volume 8 – *Life and Reign of Solomon* by Iddo the seer

Volume 9 – *The Life and Reign of Rehoboam* by Shemaiah the prophet (II Chronicles 12:15)

Volume 10 – *Life and Reign of Rehoboam* by Iddo the seer

Volume 11 – *Life and Reign of Abijah* by Iddo the seer (II Chronicles 13:22)

Volume 12 – *Life and Reign of Jehoshaphat* by Jehu the prophet (II Chronicles 20:34)

Volume 13 – *Life and Reign of Uzziah* by Isaiah the prophet (II Chronicles 26:22)

Volume 14 – *Life and Reign of Hezekiah* by Isaiah the prophet (II Chronicles 32:32-33)

*This section adapted from
The Education That Educates 155-158*

Remainder
Walking With God
'𝕬𝖓𝖉 𝕰𝖓𝖔𝖈𝖍 𝖜𝖆𝖑𝖐𝖊𝖉 𝖜𝖎𝖙𝖍 𝕲𝖔𝖉....
𝕲𝖊𝖓𝖊𝖘𝖎𝖘 5:22

Bible history left an example of what it means <u>to walk with God</u> in <u>His footprints</u>. We are told:

"Enoch's <u>walk</u> with God was not in a trance or a vision, but in <u>all the duties of his daily life.</u> He did not become a hermit, shutting himself entirely from the world; for he had a work to do for God in the world. In the family and in his intercourse with man, as a husband and father, a friend, a citizen, <u>he was the steadfast,</u> <u>unwavering servant</u> of the Lord.

"His heart was in harmony with God's will; for *'can two <u>walk</u> together, except they be agreed?'* (Amos 3:3). And this <u>holy walk</u> was continued for three hundred years. There are few Christians who would not be far more earnest and devoted if they knew that they had but a short time to live, or that the coming of Christ was about to take place. But Enoch's faith waxed the stronger, his **love** became more ardent, with the lapse of centuries.

"Enoch was a man <u>of strong and highly cultivated mind and extensive knowledge; he was honored with special revelations from God; yet being in constant communion with Heaven, with a sense of the divine greatness and perfection ever before him, he was one of the humblest of men. The closer the connection with God, the deeper was the sense of his own weakness and imperfection.</u>"

"Day by day he had longed for a closer union; nearer and nearer had grown the communion, until God took him to Himself. He had stood at the threshold of the eternal world, only <u>a step</u> between him and the land of the blest; and now the portals opened, <u>the walk with God, so long pursued on earth, continued, and he passed through the gates of the Holy City</u>—the first from among men to enter there."*

"And Enoch <u>walked</u> with God: and he was not; for God took him" (Genesis 5:24).

*Patriarchs and Prophets 85, 87

"But like Enoch, God's people will seek for purity of heart and conformity to His will, until they shall reflect the likeness of Christ. Like Enoch, they will warn the world of the Lord's second coming...."*

"We are to keep <u>walking</u> continually in the <u>footsteps</u> of Jesus, working in His lines, dispensing His gifts as good stewards of the manifold grace of God."**

*Patriarchs and Prophets 89
**I Selected Messages 191

Reinforce/Review

1. Read the chapter in *Patriarchs and Prophets*, "Seth and Enoch," pages 80-89.

2. Who were other men and women in the Bible that walked with God? (Example: *"...Noah was a just man and perfect in his generations, and Noah <u>walked</u> with God"* (Genesis 6:9). List them and a Bible text with each one, below.

_____

_____

_____

_____

_____

3. What is history? What is geography? What is prophecy?

_____

_____

_____

_____

_____

_____

_____

Reflect—"God With Us"

"Blessed is every one that feareth the LORD; that walketh in his ways."
Psalm 128:1

"...Through childhood, youth,
and manhood,
Jesus walked alone."
The Desire of Ages 92

"No one upon earth
had understood Him,
and during His ministry
He must still walk alone."
The Desire of Ages 111

"He hath showed thee,
O man, what is good;
and what doth
the LORD
require of thee,
but to do justly,
and to love mercy,
and to walk humbly
with thy God?"
Micah 6:8

"Bearing
the weakness
of humanity,
and burdened
with its sorrow and sin,
Jesus walked alone
in the midst of men."
The Desire of Ages 422

"Ministering angels
waited upon
the Lord of life
as He walked side by side
with the peasants
and laborers
among the hills
of Nazareth,
unrecognized
and unhonored."
4 Testimony 109

"Even His disciples
were so blinded
by the selfishness
of their hearts that
they were slow
to understand Him
who had come
to manifest to them
the Father's **love**.
This was why Jesus
walked in solitude
in the midst of men.
He was understood
fully in heaven alone."
The Mount of Blessing
25-26

"I will walk before the LORD
in the land of the living."
Psalm 116:9

His Mothers's Book

"Sanctify them through thy truth: thy word is truth."
John 17:17

"My mother is dying and I must go home to care for her, for she is poor and alone," said the soldier to his captain in one of the camps in Guayaquil, South America. So, although he had enlisted for three years and had served only six months, he was given permission to go home. He hurried to Cuenca, hoping to be able to save the life of his mother, but it was too late, and in spite of his care, she soon died. Then he began picking up the very few things which she owned. Most of them were in an old trunk which he found in the corner of the poor little room.

"I wonder what book this is," said the soldier, as he took a very much worn book from the bottom of the trunk. "Mother must have read it often, for it is almost falling in pieces. I will see what it tells about." He put the small book, which had no covers and many loose leaves, into his pocket while he finished the other things which he had to do.

When the room was emptied and he was lonely for the one who was gone, her book seemed like a part of his mother, so he read it over and over. Some of the things which

he found in it were very beautiful and helped him in his life, but there was a great deal which he could not understand. He wished he might find some one who could tell him what it meant. He had no idea where his mother had bought the book, and he had never seen one like it.

One day, many months later, he went into a telegraph office to see a friend and picked up a paper which his friend had been reading. The name of the paper, *Buenas Nuevas*, meaning "Good News" in English, was interesting and he began to read. Suddenly he stopped and reread a sentence. There were the very same words that he had found in his book at home.

"Where did you get this paper?" he asked his friend. "A foreigner gave it to me," answered the man. "He had many of them and gave one to whoever would take it."

"And may I borrow this for a day?" asked the soldier. "There is something here that I want to compare with a book that I have at home."

Permission being given, he took the paper to his home and then sat down with his mother's book and the paper. He found a verse in a part of his book called "Romans" and compared it with the verse which he had seen in the paper. Word for word they were the same. How happy Manuel was! He felt sure that if he could just find the man who had given out the papers, he could get help in understanding his own book.

A few days later, as he was walking down the street in Cuenca, he saw some very startling signs written on the mud walls of the town. "Down with the evangelicos or their death!" one said, and a little farther down the street was one which read, "The heads of the evangelicos or their death."

"What is an evangelico?" thought the soldier. "I must find out what the trouble is about." Soon he found a man who knew.

"A man has gone through Cuenca giving out bad papers," said the man. "He is one of those hated Christians who are spreading a false doctrine among the people of Cuenca. He must be put out of the way."

"But I must see him first," thought Manuel. "I must find out what he knows of my book." So he hurried down the street to find the house where the man was staying with two other Christians. He went to the door, but a policeman in plain clothes was stationed there to prevent a foreigner from being killed in Cuenca. The man could be run out of town, but there must be no violence, and he refused to let Manuel in. Again and again Manuel tried, saying that he had come as a friend. At last his patience was rewarded and he was allowed to get into the house where the missionary was staying. He told of his errand, showed his mother's book, and asked for help.

What a wonderful day that was in Manuel's life! For more than three hours he sat with the missionary, listening to the story of Christ's life, of his friendship with the men of Palestine, and of the book called the Bible which told of His life and work.

"And it is part of that book—the latter part—which you have from your mother," said the missionary. "It is the greatest book in the world."

Mark Your Bible
Prophecies Relating to Christ's First Advent

**Christ was portrayed not by one,
but by twenty or twenty-five artists (or prophets)
none of whom had ever seen the Man they were painting.**

1. God inspired the prophets to foretell the truth carefully and accurately.

Jeremiah 1:12 – *"Then said the LORD unto me, Thou hast well seen: for I will hasten my word to perform it."*

2. God gave the first prophecy about the birth of Christ.

Genesis 3:15 – *"And I will put enmity* [hostility and hatred] *between thee and the woman, and between thy seed and her seed; it shall bruise thy head, and thou shalt bruise his heel."*

Note: Satan was the first to learn of a Deliverer. From this point on we follow the promises and prophecies (like footprints) concerning *"the seed of the woman"* and the path lengthens until it ends in the birth of Christ.

3. Mary is chosen to be Jesus' mother.

Matthew 1:18 – *"Now the birth of Jesus Christ was on this wise: When as his mother Mary was espoused to Joseph, before they came together, she was found with child of the Holy Ghost."*

4. Mary was of the house of David.

Romans 1:3 – *"Concerning his son Jesus Christ our Lord, which was made of the seed of David according to the flesh."*

5. It was prophesied that Jesus would be born of a virgin.

Isaiah 7:14 – *"Therefore the Lord himself shall give you a sign; Behold, a virgin shall conceive, and bear a son, and shall call his name Immanuel."*

Note: Jesus did not have an earthly father, but a heavenly Father. Joseph became His step-father. Mary was a young unmarried woman who had preserved the purity of her body.

6. It was written in Scripture when the Baby was to be born.

Daniel 9:25 – *"Know therefore and understand, that from the going forth of the commandment to restore and to build Jerusalem, unto the Messiah the Prince, shall be seven weeks, and threescore and two weeks...."*

7. Jesus was born on time.

Galatians 4:4 – *"But when the fulness of the time was come, God sent forth his Son, made of a woman, made under the law."*

Note: As the time of His birth drew near, Mary was actually living at the wrong place if her Son, the Messiah, was to be born in Bethlehem of Judea. But God knows the future and fulfills His prophetic Word.

In 1923 there was discovered at Ankara, Turkey, a Roman temple inscription which stated that in the reign of Caesar Augustus there were three great tax collections. The second was ordered four years before the birth of Christ; the third, several years after His birth.

The second special tax was the one the proud Jews resented; so they sent a commission to Rome to protest about it. The commission finally failed; the Jews had to submit to the enrollment and taxing.

8. A decree went forth from Caesar Augustus for taxes.

Luke 2:1 – *"And it came to pass in those days, that there went out a decree from Caesar Augustus, that all the world should be taxed."*

Note: By the time the official tax collectors had worked their way eastward, town by town, and after the time-consuming delays caused by the Jewish protests, exactly enough delay was caused, and all in the natural course of events, so that when the enrollment was put in force in Judea the exact time had come for Mary to give birth to her Child.

9. Christ's name was a description of His mission on this earth.

Isaiah 7:14 – *"...And shall call his name Immanuel."*

Matthew 1:23 – *"...And they shall call his name Emmanuel, which being interpreted is, <u>God with us</u>."*

Outline of School Program

Age	Grade	Program
Birth through Age 7	Babies Kindergarten and Pre-school	*Family Bible Lessons* (This includes: Bible, Science–Nature, and Character)
Age 8	First Grade	*Family Bible Lessons* (This includes: Bible, Science–Nature, and Character) + Language Program (*Writing and Spelling Road to Reading and Thinking* [WSRRT])
Age 9-14 or 15	Second through Eighth Grade	*The Desire of all Nations* (This includes: Health, Mathematics, Music, Science–Nature, History/Geography/Prophecy, Language, and Voice–Speech) + Continue using WSRRT
Ages 15 or 16-19	Ninth through Twelfth Grade	9 – *Cross and Its Shadow I** + Appropriate Academic Books 10 – *Cross and Its Shadow II** + Appropriate Academic Books 11 – *Daniel the Prophet** + Appropriate Academic Books 12 – *The Seer of Patmos** (Revelation) + Appropriate Academic Books *or you could continue using *The Desire of Ages*
Ages 20-25	College	Apprenticeship

Made in the USA
Las Vegas, NV
26 September 2021